BREWERY RAILWAYS

IAN P. PEATY

DAVID & CHARLES
Newton Abbot   London   North Pomfret (Vt)

ACKNOWLEDGMENTS

The author is indebted to so many people who have generously loaned photographs and given information over the many years of enjoyable research and collection of material in compiling this book. Most of the brewers and malting companies have given me assistance and this is gratefully acknowledged. Special thanks are expressed to fellow members of the Industrial Railway Society, particularly Jim Peden, also Nigel Bowdidge of the Historical Model Railway Society. To Robin Atthill and F. R. Warwick and the staff of the Bass Burton Museum go my thanks. Were it not for the foresight of such excellent photographers as Ivo Peters, and Dr Ian C. Allen, whose reminiscences of the East Anglian railway scene have given me such pleasure, this book would not have been possible, nor indeed without the encouragement, assistance and loan of his own considerable photographic collection, from R. C. Riley to whom go my greatest thanks. My appreciation is also recorded for the excellent photographic quality produced from often poor archive material by Mike Johnson, also to Carol Austin and Pat Collins for typing the manuscript. To my friends in Arthur Guinness & Son at Park Royal brewery, my grateful thanks for the pleasant hours enjoyed photographing the last operational brewery railway system. Lastly, my appreciation for permission to use material and photographs and assistance given by colleagues within the Allied Breweries group, particularly past and present friends at the Romford Brewery. The persons and companies who have loaned pictures and given information are:

Associated British Maltsters Ltd, Albrew Maltsters Ltd, Bass Charrington Ltd, Benskins, Brewers Society, Burton Daily Mail, Burton Brewery Company, S. Briggs & Company, Cargill-Albion Ltd, Courage, P. B. Ltd, Essex County Council, A. Guinness & Son, Dublin, A. Guinness & Son, Park Royal, Industrial Railway Society, Newark District Council Museum, Irish Railway Record Society, Marston, Thompson & Evershed Ltd, Mitchell & Butler Ltd, National Railway Museum, Romford Brewery Company, Samuel Webster & Sons Ltd, Scottish & Newcastle Breweries Ltd, Suffolk County Council, Tetley Walker Ltd, Truman, Hanbury & Buxton Ltd, Watney, Combe Reid Ltd, Whitbread Flowers Ltd, Wiggin Richardson, Wrexham Lager Brewery Company, Ordnance Survey Maps.

Messrs I. Garwood, K. Garwood, M. Berry, C. E. Lee, M. D. Hardy, C. Reilly, F. W. Shuttleworth, F. Jones, R. Prince, J. Watling, H. Richards, D. Murray, W. F. Carty, and Major J. A. Hibbert.

British Library Cataloguing in Publication Data

Peaty, Ian P.
  Brewery railways.
  1. Railways, Industrial – Great Britain –
  History 2. Brewing industry – Great
  Britain – History
  I. Title
  385'.54'0941   HE3816

ISBN 0–7153–8605–0

© Ian P. Peaty 1985

Photoset by Northern Phototypesetting Co, Bolton and printed in Great Britain by Biddles Limited, Guildford, Surrey for David & Charles (Publishers) Limited Brunel House Newton Abbot Devon

Published in the United States of America by David & Charles Inc North Pomfret Vermont 05053 USA

Contents

1
The Brewing, Malting and Hop Industries

The brewing of beer is one of the oldest known occupations, with evidence that the ancient Egyptians were indulging in its manufacture. In this country it was also one of the first activities to transform from a purely home-based operation to a factory process. It is recorded that in 1419, London boasted no fewer than 300 breweries, but with the massive escalation in the population in the Victorian era brewing had become almost totally industrialised. Before this growth, most farmers brewed beer and cider for themselves and their farmhands, with large country houses brewing their own beer for the wealthy families and staff. Many publicans, too, were brewing for their customers, until they were absorbed rapidly into the tied house system by developing brewing companies. During these affluent Victorian times there were public houses being built on almost every street corner of every town. Unlike the present day when nearly all public houses have a full licence, allowing them to sell beers, wines and spirits, in Victorian times and even right up to the mid-1950s, many pubs were licensed either for beer only, or wines and spirits. Just as there were numerous public houses, there were equally proportionately many more breweries than exist today. County towns would have three or four each, and as an example the county of Cambridgeshire in the late 19th century had no fewer than thirty breweries, this being the largest industry after agriculture, with brickmaking being the next most labour-intensive employment.

Before the brewer commences his masterful art, he must have the required raw materials. The basis of the brewing process is the mixture of boiling water, or as the brewer calls it liquor, to malt in order to extract a saccharine solution, then by the addition of hops by which the aromatic bitter is extracted, to convert the solution into a fermented beverage. Malt is first crushed between cylindrical rollers, so adjusted to break every corn. When crushed, the malt is called grist; it is then pumped to a mashing tun where it is mixed with the boiling water, the mixture is then known as wort. From the tun the wort flows into the underback and then into the copper, where the hops are added to the boiling mixture until it reaches the required specific gravity. The wort is then let off into the hop back, from where it is pumped into the cooler. The hop back has a perforated false bottom through which the wort runs, leaving the spent hops to be disposed of. The coolers were large shallow vessels, usually copper lined, situated at the top of the building with louvred walls and roof clerestory to allow the steam to dissipate and the liquid to cool. Later developments dispensed with this primitive system by using paraflow coolers and refrigerators. The cooled wort then flows into the fermenting tuns where the yeast is added, and the fermentation ensues. When complete, the yeast is skimmed off; we now have alcoholic beer. The final stage prior to dispatch to the public house is for the beer to be racked into casks, or if it is to be bottled it is pasteurised before it is bottled by hand or machine. Cask-conditioned beers have a secondary fermentation which takes place in the public house after finings have been added just prior to delivery. Lagers use different strains of yeast which act on the wort at the bottom of the fermenting vessels, they are then chilled and filtered, as are brewery conditioned, or 'keg' beers.

Breweries and maltings alike are architecturally distinctive, with several features designed to carry out the smooth daily function of their industries. In earlier breweries common in all towns, the design was arranged around the tower system, in which the raw materials were hoisted or pumped to the highest point, and then the remaining process descended by gravitation, finally finishing with the beer being stored in cellars. In the case of the several larger breweries, particularly those of Burton-on-Trent, a horizontal system employing pumps was used. With the inevitable growth of these larger breweries, they very soon ran out of room, hence the many separate sites of several breweries in the town of Burton. Subsequently these different sites had to be connected by transport, as each site specialised in different aspects of the brewing and malting process. As with corn mills, provision was made in breweries and maltings alike for lifting the sacks of grain or malt from incoming transport to the top of the building in order that the grain could be either stored or fed through the brewing process. This facility is best carried out by the dormer type housing which protrudes from the roof elevations called a 'lucam'. Housed inside was a pulley and chains used to pull up the sacks; the floor of the lucam consisted of two upward opening flaps with a central hole to allow the chain to pass through, thereby allowing the sacks to be drawn up through the flaps which then immediately close shut for safety. An excellent example of a typical country town steam brewery is the now preserved All Saints Brewery at Stamford, Lincolnshire. This is a delightfully unspoilt Victorian brewery which is now a museum open to the public, and it is possible to see and understand the entire brewing process, stage by stage.

An architectural feature which remained popular with brewery owners was the use of Georgian motifs,

The entire area beneath the passenger platforms at St Pancras Station, London, was devoted to the storage of beer. (C. E. Lee)

especially in the use of round-headed windows with iron frames and ornamental contrasting brickwork. This was even extended to the elaborate oversailing and bell-mouthed brickwork to the top of the prolific chimney stacks. Architects were well aware that brewers wished to project to their customers a feeling of quality, longevity, and prosperity, just as banking companies have always done. Layout plans of breweries have had to give major prominence to accessibility by transport in the siting of most buildings, within the confines of the departmental sequence, in the case of the very large companies, to railways as well as road. Due to restrictions imposed by many town sites, buildings often had to be built in close proximity to each other, and where served by railway sidings, these were of exceptionally sharp curves, and in the tightest of conditions, liberal use was made of wagon turntables.

The deep loam soils of East Anglia coupled with the temperate North Sea breezes and soft mists help to ripen the high quality barley, the richest in the land. So it is natural that throughout this part of the land, many maltings, both large and small, are to be found. The larger maltings obviously required adequate transport facilities, and as with the growth of railways, so many new and larger maltings were built in the 1840s, alongside railways and creeks and rivers. In the small

Hertfordshire town of Sawbridgeworth, the maltings of several firms were built alongside the canal and beside the railway. The Stort Navigation provided a direct link into the London breweries; regrettably neither the canal nor the railway provide the means of transport on which these maltings once depended and around which they were built.

The opening of the River Stort to navigation in 1769 commenced the decline of malting in the town of Saffron Walden, 20 miles further inland on the Essex/Cambridge county boundary. This decline at Saffron Walden was typical of many malting towns not served by water or rail connections. The poor road surfaces were unable to withstand the considerable volume of carts, which formed huge ruts and caused considerable delays. So it was that the malt was unable to get to the London breweries in prime condition. The town of Bishop's Stortford at the head of the Stort Navigation, a spur off the Lea Valley Navigation, became the malting centre, with some 100 maltings. Because of the opening-up of that town, Saffron

5

Walden's business lost 29 maltings in the seventeen years between 1831 and 1848.

A proposal in the late 18th Century to extend the Stort Navigation to link with the river Cam at Cambridge was thwarted by Lord Howard of Audley End, as it would have traversed his recently-renovated estate. However, the Northern & Eastern Railway, (later the Eastern Counties Railway) constructed its main line between London and Cambridge with two castellated portico tunnel entrances within the estate grounds. This line reached Bishop's Stortford on 16 May 1842, thereby dramatically improving the transhipment of malt into London's breweries, and no doubt to the more local large brewery at Romford. The Victorian industrial revolution even influenced the most rural areas with the growing transport network of canals and railways, helping to slake the thirst of the growing nation in its halcyon days.

As with other development businesses in the Industrial Revolution, malting underwent its own changes. Small-scale production was carried on by four or five men, working under their pyramid roofs and

Turn of the century at Selling, as a trainload of East London hop pickers disembark from an assortment of SECR coaches (*Courage*)

wooden cowls in very small buildings, some of which may still be seen today. As with brewing, strong men with muscle and brawn were the hallmark of the trade. The revolution came with the 'big is beautiful' theme, incorporating all the latest technological innovations. But despite these modern methods of mechanical malting, the traditional broad wooden malt shovels and rakes were still to be found in use right up to the 1960s.

On arrival at the maltings, the grain is off-loaded from the farmers' vehicles or the larger maltings own fleet. At the large maltings, served by either rail or water, large consignments come in loose form, requiring pipework on gantries. Otherwise the grain is conveyed in sacks, and is then selected and graded, samples of each consignment being sent to the laboratories for grading and moisture testing.

In the process of converting the grain into malt, the barley is dried to a degree which will allow storage without any deterioration, as it may be in store for up to six months. The harvest which takes place during the months of September and October makes the autumn a very busy time of the year for the malster and his transport manager.

The grain passes through several mills in order to remove dust, grit and chaff. It is then stored on the top floors of buildings which are sometimes eight storeys

high. When required the grain is fed by gravity through tanks of water; the wet grain is then spread evenly over vast areas of floors. The wheat germinates, and it is then roasted and malt is produced, after much 'ploughing' to turn the green malt, or 'piece' as it is known. The malt is then weighed into sacks for delivery by road, rail or water. To ensure that the quality is maintained the malt must be most carefully looked after, with close sheeting-up in tarpaulins in the case of road and water transit. When it was moved by rail, special covered ventilated vans or grain wagons were used, with overhead hopper loading into the vans and discharge at the bottom between the rails. When the malt reached the brewer, be it in the early days by horse-drawn wagon or nowadays by giant articulated lorries, it was sieved, milled and broken-down into a fine gritty consistency called 'grist'. It was then ready for the brewer to brew, after its long journey from the farmers' autumn harvest.

A traditional malting was designed so that the barley grain was hoisted up to the top floor via a lucam, then it was fed by gravity into the cistern or 'steep' for a few days, allowing the grain to swell. It was then drained and spread on a perforated floor known as the 'couch', where it was laid out evenly to a depth of a few inches. Here it lay for about a week, while it was regularly turned and racked with wooden tools, steadily germinating.

At the critical stage the germination was arrested by exposure to heat from the kiln, sited at one end of the building. This was always at the opposite end to the cistern, with two or three long floors between each to accommodate for the large areas required for the grain. The earliest maltings had round kilns with cowls, very similar to the Kent hop oast houses, but the prolific growth from 1840 onwards made use of slates which were more suited to the rectangular pyramidal shape, topped with a louvred flue. To take the great weight of

The South Eastern & Chatham Railway handled vast quantities of hops destined for the Southwark Hop Market and London breweries. (*Author's Collection*)

the wet grain on several floors, cast-iron columns came into common use from about the same period. The external appearance of these long, low, buildings consisted of superimposed regular brick buttresses with tie-irons, often of a florid decorative nature and with the local ironfounder's name and date. Between these buttresses there were segmented and louvred windows, often painted white; sometimes these were supplemented by shutters in order to cut out the light seeping into the usual six-foot headroom of each floor. This was to enable the maltster to control the germination of the grain. A lucam was provided and all maltings of more than one floor have been replaced by grain elevators. Some lucams have had a disproportionate expense put into them, as evidenced by elaborate carved corbals and braces or intricate cast-iron spandrels. The usual horizontal timber boarding was inevitably painted white and contrasted starkly against the slate roofs; in larger maltings served by rail sidings often several lucams overhanging the track were in evidence. The bold and often grand scale of malthouses, with their interesting skylines punctuated with truncated-cone kiln flues, even today gives evidence of their past occupation – fortunately many interesting examples still remain to be seen throughout East Anglia. These large buildings however hide the fact that the number of men who worked in them were comparatively few, and very disproportionate to a similar sized building devoted to industrial manufacturing.

Because of the seasonal nature of workers in the malt industry in the 19th century, and the clay soil which is

7

Thameside dock shunting at Woolwich at the Albion Sugar Company's factory, one of several specialist suppliers of brewers sugars. (*Cargill/Albion*)

both suitable for growing barley and for brick and tile making, there are numerous instances of close association between workers of the two industries. The malting season commenced in September and continued through the winter and early spring months, when many of the workers would be laid-off. With the improving spring weather, the wet working conditions in the open clay pits allowed for digging the clay, and so many of the men were able to continue in employment during the late spring and summer months, making bricks and tiles.

There are numerous locations where these two industries worked harmoniously side by side. The railway sidings which served Flower's Brewery at Stratford-on-Avon passed through the brewery and crossed a main road into a large brickworks; this was later infilled and at the time of the brewery closure in 1971; part of the brickfield was the brewery's motor vehicle department. At Bures, Suffolk, a small brickworks was immediately adjacent to the railway maltings owned by Truman, Hanbury & Buxton. Likewise at Long Melford, Suffolk, Braintree, and Thorpe-le-Soken, Essex, brickworks were in close attendance to the maltings. At Sudbury, Suffolk and at Thurrock, Essex, breweries and maltings were sharing their labour with chalk workings in the case at Sudbury. These chalk pits were owned by the Great Eastern Railway Company, which had a siding serving the works.

Hops were introduced into this country by the Dutch in the late 16th century, with Kent being selected as the most suitable area because of its enclosed field system, suitable soil and a ready supply of timber for poles and charcoal. This early influence by the Dutch is still recognised to this day by the names given to the sizes of beer casks, Kilderkin for 18 gallons and Firkin for 9 gallons. The beverage produced by the English before the introduction of hops was called ale, and since the introduction of hops it is now known as beer. The first hop market was established in Little Eastcheap, London, and later moved to the Borough in South-East London. In 1774 an Act of Parliament required all hop sacks to be marked with the grower's name, place and year, and very soon each farmer adopted his own symbol, with the rampant horse of Kent becoming prominent. In 1800 there were 35,000 acres of hops under cultivation, reaching a peak of 71,789 acres in 1878, with no fewer than 40 English counties, 8 Welsh and 5 Scottish counties growing the hop vine.

In 1932 the Hops Marketing Board was created. Two years later the first hop-picking machine was introduced at Suckley in Worcestershire. At that time the cost of hand picking a bushel was 2/6d (12½p), but by the new machines the cost was reduced to 4d (2p). Because of the onset of World War II, the machines presented no threat to the many thousands of hop pickers until well into the 1950s. By far the most popular variety with brewers is the Fuggles variety as this has a high alpha count, giving improved bittering qualities, but newer varieties such as Wye Target are gaining in popularity. The hop picking families usually visited the same farms, often one generation after another, but were often disliked by the locals, because of their swearing and drunkenness. The famous Whitbread hop farm at Beltring, with its 25 cowls, in three blocks, set in 300 acres of the beautiful Weald of Kent, produced half a million bushels of hops, which in the 1930s took 5,000 workers to pick in the short autumn season.

In Kent where three-fifths of all English hops are grown, the circular building used for drying the hops are called oast houses; in Hereford and Worcestershire they are known as kells. The flower of the female hop, or cone, is the part of the climbing vine that the brewer requires. At the base of each bracteole there is a small seed which is high in oil content; it is this oil or resin that provides the necessary aroma and bitterness, also the tannin content that helps to clarify the final product. Hops are gathered in late summer, and then dried in the traditional oast houses, with their circular brick buildings topped by cone-shaped roofs with cowls. This cowl is pivoted and is always provided with a vane, often of a decorative shape, which keeps the top opening turned away from the wind. The hops are spread on the floor about 2ft deep above the kiln, and when ready they are then moved to the cooling loft. The dried hops are then shovelled into long hessian sacks suspended under the floor, where the hops are compressed into the pockets, which weigh $1\frac{1}{2}$ cwt, with the neck being sewn with two hand holds. These are then dropped to the ground floor for storage until they are dispatched to the breweries. Referring to Charles Dickens in his *Pickwick Papers*, Mr Jingle retorts, "Kent, Sir? Everybody knows Kent – apples, cherries, hops and women!" The Garden of England has all the qualities justly to make this claim!

Beside malt and hops used in the production of beer, yeast and molasses are also required to complete the conversion of sugar to alcohol. Yeast is a micro-organism of a creamy colour, which is very active in certain temperatures in which it needs careful control, this being achieved by a reduction in temperature. It can behave in an erratic manner, particularly if it should come into contact with strains of wild yeast. These are found in the air, as witnessed by the action on the skin of damaged fruit, such as apples or grapes going mouldy. The yeast in the air will act and start fermentation, just as the brewer requires, but essentially under his control. Different yeast strains are cultivated by the various breweries, some of which have been in use continuously for many years. Because it is so prolific in its action, there is always a surplus after each brew and this is sold to firms which utilise it in medicinal and food products. Many breweries allowed local housewives and employees to take home sufficient yeast for their own home baking.

The sugar content in malt is supplemented by the addition of molasses to assist in the conversion process to alcohol, also to provide the requisite amount of sweetness in certain beers, particularly dark mild. Several specialist firms provide these brewers' molasses – likewise there are firms which deal in spent hops and grains. These residual products are high in protein and consequently are of great value to farmers, as easily digestible animal foodstuff. In between this complete cycle the brewer has used the farmers' produce to make his beer. At every stage, from the farmer harvesting his crop, to the maltster, to the brewer to the customer, transport, in many forms, has played its essential part.

The Brewer's business is as old and rich in tradition as history itself; a slow and gentle art. It has given pleasure to life, it has strengthened resolve, it has softened sorrow. Countless millions have enjoyed its nourishment and its ability to break down social barriers, so much so that the English pub is an integral part of our heritage, a haven from this troubled world.

2

The Railway Transport of Beer, Malt, Hops and Yeast

From the disastrous rail strike of 1963, the volumes of freight for the licensed trade have decreased dramatically. With the massive cut-backs of branch lines by the late Lord Beeching, the local goods yard or private siding where single wagons could be loaded and unloaded became a scene of the past. With the modern freight-handling equipment came improved wagon designs to cope with larger loads and higher traffic speeds. On the formation of British Railways on 1 January 1948 from the four main line companies, modernisation programmes became of increasing relevance. During the 1960s some attempt was made by British Rail to get back some of the previous lucrative brewery business which it had enjoyed prior to the 1950s. Fork-lift trucks were coming into general use in all industries, with the wooden pallet being the unit of transit for both road and rail. To accommodate this pallet traffic, British Rail converted 4-wheel long-wheelbase tube wagons, which carried two rows of seven pallets each, with each pallet holding 18 kegs of beer. Ind Coope's Burton and Wrexham Breweries were the first to use this service, the 'Ale Pallet' traffic terminating in London. There were several variants of wagon in use, with Bass/Worthington soon following Ind Coope's lead in late 1965. British Railways traffic census taken on 23 April 1961, indicated 0.3 million tons of beer and 1.4 million tons of grain (this latter figure included wheat/flour for the baking industry).

Grain traffic had been handled in 20-ton bulk grain hopper vans (BGV) since the mid-1930s, and finally the last of some 400 wagons succumbed in 1982! These 'hoppers' were to be seen throughout the Eastern Counties, from Essex into Scotland where they were often to be seen delivering their loads to remote whisky distilleries. The volume in 1980 amounted to only 0.5 million tons, due to the very limited siding facilities. The *Speedlink* concept of fast and reliable freight trains between some 30 terminal points throughout Britain, controlled by the TOPS computer at British Rail headquarters allows train speeds of 60mph, with full wagon utilisation. At the same time, BR once again encouraged the use of private-owner wagons, so a new company was formed to handle bulk loads, Traffic Services Ltd. Using continental design 57-ton 4-axle Polybulk Grainflow wagons, able to handle between 100,000 and 250,000 tons per year on several routes, the service came on stream in 1981. If several of the large breweries and malting companies can be

persuaded to reconnect their premises with BR metals, the enormous potential of both grain and beer coming back onto railways is a distinct possibility. Faced with increasing fuel and labour costs by road transport the future of BR's freight in this industry could be encouraging.

The century-long tradition by Arthur Guinness of using railways for its distribution continues to this day, indicating that rail transit of beer can be carried out in a viable manner. In Ireland the national rail system, CIE, has adapted with the brewery to the latest methods of fast bulk handling. In 1968, 200 Lancashire Flats with ISO latching, with a capacity of 90 Guinness Kegs in two tiers, were brought into use for journeys to Cork, Galway, Limerick, Sligo and Waterford. For the important export trade, primarily to Belgium via Waterford and Rotterdam, ISO tanks are used. In addition to the ISO tanks, circular 504-gallon transportable tanks are used for the Northern Irish beer traffic and to the Isle of Man. The supply of grain to the St James' Gate brewery in Dublin comes from a supplier in County Cork, the barley being transported northward in 20ft ISO hopper containers.

As far as it has been able to ascertain, the London brewers Whitbread, used railways only to a very small extent. In 1939, the LMS Derby workshops built five 10ft wheelbase trucks to carry 4-wheel road tankers, followed in 1946 with a further ten. These had white lettering on the single bauxite painted side rail: '10t LMS. Shunt with care. For use of Whitbread's tanks only'. These vehicles were in use between London and Chester, but were also probably used on the Continental export trade on the Southern Region of British Railways, working out of Nine Elms to Southampton. In the 1950s six 22-ton Conflat LT long wheelbase wagons came into use to carry $8\frac{1}{4}$-ton road/rail aluminium alloy bulk malt tanks for the newly-formed Scottish & Newcastle Breweries Ltd. These containers were built by Carmichael of Worcester and had two filling hatches on top with a single bottom discharge; the unit was lifted by a crane from the rail wagon onto a 3-axle platform lorry at each railhead. These six bulk malt tanks were used between Edinburgh and Gateshead, just south of the River Tyne at Newcastle, travelling on the east coast route via Ashington, Berwick and Dunbar, and were exclusively for this brewery's traffic.

To give some idea of 'brewery traffic' throughout the

country, I have taken a selection of this activity, commencing in Scotland and working southward, incorporating some further details of one or two specific breweries, and the movement of products in this industry.

William McEwan & Co Ltd, the famous Edinburgh brewer has its Fountain Brewery sited alongside the Glasgow–Edinburgh main line, sandwiched between Dundee Street and the railway which served the brewery and bottling hall for seventy years or more. Before 1900, McEwan was one of fourteen Edinburgh breweries served by their own private railway sidings, half of which were served originally by the North British Railway, the remainder by the Caledonian Railway.

Prior to 1890, the production of the Fountain Brewery was between 1,000 and 1,500 barrels per day for local trade, with 400 to 500 barrels for export. The export trade was of great importance – the 'Export' quality in its scarlet can continues today as a major part of the portfolio of Scottish & Newcastle Breweries Ltd. Bottled beers were of great importance in this export trade, with bottling halls at Edinburgh and Glasgow devoted entirely for export trade, the home trade being carried out by outside bottling firms. All bottles used for export were in fact imported. The trade to Cuba was packaged in earthenware bottles. Wooden cases and barrels were used for packing bottles, between 5,000 and 6,000 cases being made per month. The American and Antilles trade preferred bottled light and dark beers packed with straw in barrels rather than cases. The product, which was to become known almost throughout the world, was the 'Globe' brand.

The Fountain Brewery was served by six sidings, the last being installed in the early 1950s for the boiler house; this had an enclosed coal intake hopper feeder which distributed fuel at high level to the boiler house, an ash hopper being situated alongside the siding for the waste products. The four boilers were installed by John Thompson Ltd of Glasgow the coal handling and storage plant was supplied by Robert Boby Ltd of Bury St Edmunds, the well-known malt machinery manufacturer. A further siding served the bottle case storage sheds, with a long siding serving the middle

One of the special beer trains leaving Burton-on-Trent for St Pancras, London on 11 December 1929, with 28 specialised beer vans hauled by LMS Class 4F 0–6–0 No. 4432, passing the former Midland Railway locomotive shed. (*National Railway Museum*)

section of the brewery which housed the bottled beer dispatch department. Next came a siding which curved into the heart of the brewery, terminating at the cooperage and cask-washing shed and storage yard. The final set of two sidings served the rail tanker filling dock. Supplies of beer were sent to the Glasgow depot by six conventional rail tankers of 68-barrel capacity EMP glass-lined Pfaudler tanks, specially insulated. In addition to these tank wagons introduced in the early 1950s, a further six Dyson trailer road tankers hauled by ERF. 'Cobs' kept up a continuous daily supply to Glasgow; the road tankers eventually were to oust the rail transit. The railway tank wagons were resplendent with their red 'McEwan's for Quality' followed by 'Brewed in Edinburgh for bottling in Glasgow, by William McEwan Co Ltd, Fountain Brewery Edinburgh', in black on a white background.

In Scotland the several railway companies provided special open slatted high-sided wagons for the cask beer trade, primarily between Glasgow and Edinburgh, but with northern trade extending beyond Perth up to Inverness. The old Glasgow & South Western Railway had long-wheelbase wagons of 6-ton capacity, with the North British building a 10-ton 'empty cask' wagon in 1890. Later larger versions were built in 1908, these returning to South Leith or Kirkcaldy when empty Several of these survived in use by the LNER, albeit of the 12-ton capacity, in the Southern Scottish area and border country to Newcastle. Alloa is situated at the head of the Firth of Forth and is an important brewing town specialising in lager, the penchant of the Scots. Considerable rail-borne beer traffic emanated from this small town, chiefly going south via Carlisle to Burton-on-Trent, and south to Southampton for export bottling.

Three Scottish maltings served by rail sidings, in

11

Modern Grainflow polybulk wagons on the Airdrie branch, propelled by Associated British Malsters ex-BR Class 08 diesel, in chocolate brown livery with orange 'ears of barley' logo. (*ABM*).

Fifeshire at Kirkcaldy, Ladybank and Thornton Junction, looking across to the south bank of the Firth of Forth to Leith, were all served by the North British Railway, as was the large malting at Airdrie, to the east of Glasgow and Coatbridge. A short branch line of single track traversed a wooded area to the malting which is now part of the country's largest malting combine, ABM. A former BR Class 08 diesel painted in the company's eye-catching brown livery, six orange stripes with broad fantail giving a modern representation of ears of barley, works 50-ton TSL Grainflow polybulk bogie wagons to the malting, believed to be the first and last case of a malting company using its own locomotive. A very large volume of the malt produced in Scotland from locally-grown barley is still used in that nation's premier spirit, but there has always been sufficient production to satisfy the needs of local breweries.

Of the numerous large Midlands brewery companies other than those of Burton-on-Trent it is interesting to record the rail traffic of Peter Walker & Son of Warrington whose prime business other than locally within the town was in the Liverpool area; this necessitated a considerable east-west rail traffic, contrary to the general trend of north-south beer traffic.

In the 1820s Peter Walker founded a small brewery in Liverpool, having removed from his native burgh of Ayr. His name is immortalised in the brewing trade by his introduction of what is now known as the 'Burton Union System' for cleansing the beer of yeast. By 1846 his second son had commenced brewing in Warrington,

but after a few years of massively increased business, he removed to new premises at Dallam Lane, the present brewery occupying this site. The road of this name divided the brewery from the branch line of the LNWR, also of the same name, this being opened as early as 25 July 1831. From an early date the brewery was served by three wagon turntables which passed over Dallam Lane into the brewery, whereupon two of the single sidings split into numerous sidings, loops and spurs serving all parts of the brewery. The brewery turntables were surrounded by several others, also private sidings which served numerous steel and wire works and forges. The Dallam branch of the Warrington & Newton Railway was unique in that one of Walker's public houses, the 'Three Pigeons Inn', served as a booking office and waiting room.

Inward rail traffic consisted of some five coal wagons per day, with malt vans continuing to arrive from the Eastern Counties up until February 1978, by which time the brewery was part of the vast Allied Breweries organisation. Each wagon was brought from the railway turntables by the brewery's own tractor unit and earlier by two of the brewery heavy horses. Outward traffic consisted of Walker's noted 'Mild', this product still being popular in the Midlands, whereas similar dark beers in the South have lost greatly in favour. Pale and India Ales were produced at Walker's Midland Brewery at Burton-on-Trent, established at Shobnall in 1877, these products being transported by rail northward via Stoke-on-Trent to the Warrington Brewery and Liverpool stores. Each evening a 'Walker's Special' goods train left the Dallam Lane branch with its precious cargo of 'Walker's Ale', destined for the Park Lane Stores of the LNWR. At the turn of the century this amounted to 10,000 barrels weekly, with a second Liverpool store being used at

Crown Street. Several large hydraulic cranes were situated in the covered and pedimented Park Lane Stores to handle this large volume. Below the siding and ale unloading bank were situated cavernous brick vaults which held 3,000 barrels. These vaults were emptied daily, casks being lifted up to the ground level by hoists, and loaded onto the same rail wagons which had brought the full beer casks in the night before. Beer traffic was also dispatched to Walker's own siding serving its Chester depot in Tramway Street, this movement continuing up until 1955. Beer was also sent via Chester to Holyhead, passing over the famous Menai Bridge connecting North Wales with Anglesey.

To the east of the heavily populated and industrialised areas of Manchester, Stoke-on-Trent, Sheffield and Nottingham lies the sparsely populated agricultural county of Lincoln. Maltings served by railway sidings were numerous within the county, stretching from Grantham, Sleaford and Boston in the south, Louth, Lincoln and Newark in the centre. The latter town was the heart of the malt industry, importing and exporting barley and malt via the Immingham Docks on the Humber. These were built by the Great Central Railway in 1912 to handle coal and grain, and were opened formally by King George V on 22nd July 1912, at which time he knighted Sam Fay, the GCR's General Manager. The docks continue to handle large quantities of grain, particularly for the ABM group, alas not by rail. The same company's malting at Louth was the sole reason for the truncated route of the old GNR to continue in use in BR days, but this traffic had to eventually close as unviable. Further north the county of Yorkshire also had its share of numerous maltings with railway sidings, with W. J. Robson's malting at Pontefract being one of the few maltings in the country which had its own privately-owned coal wagons. Because of the dramatic difference in population between East and West Midlands, between agriculture and industry, the rail traffic of malt travelled westward, with a much reduced beer traffic in return, particularly from the great breweries of Burton-on-Trent.

In North Wales, beer rail traffic intersected at Connah's Quay, with much East-West traffic coming and going to Holyhead for the Irish trade. Large quantities of Guinness Stout exported from Dublin for the Midlands area came via this route, destined for the Guinness Depot in Liverpool, where the considerable Irish population ensured a continued demand. In the reverse direction several breweries in the Liverpool, Warrington and Manchester areas enjoyed a reciprocal trade. The north–south traffic chiefly came from Wrexham where several breweries made use of the railway network, most notable being the Wrexham Lager Brewery which sent its lagers to Liverpool and Southampton docks for the passenger liner business. Five miles south of Connah's Quay, the Lassell & Charman Brewery at Caergwrle had its own rail siding for transporting its beers to the Liverpool and Birkenhead areas, with a further siding at Cefn-y-bedd.

The coal mining area of South Wales had its share of breweries to slake the thirst of miners, and two utilised the old Rhymney Railway to transport their beer – the Pengam and the Brynmawr Breweries, situated in the heart of the mining valleys. Of the few maltings in Wales which had railway sidings, that of Phillips situated in the Alexandra Docks at Newport was able to supply the local breweries around Swansea and Cardiff. Phillips' maltings were ideally placed to receive the barley imported from America, with the finished malt only requiring short distances of rail transport to the breweries. Because of the very dense railway network in South Wales, built to bring the coal down the valleys to the docks for export, the Welsh breweries were able to take advantage of the railways, whereas the short distances would not have normally warranted such transport usage.

Welsh coal is well renowned, but it may not be fully appreciated that with its many varieties, qualities and grades, the coal was also used for specialist brewing purposes. Anthracite mined in the Swansea area was particularly suitable for malting and hop-drying kilns, with several collieries advertising 'Big Vein' on their wagons, which travelled from their home metals of the Great Western and Neath & Brecon Railways, to those in the Southern and Eastern Counties. Closer to home in the Severn Valley the GWR enjoyed a northern flow of loaded anthracite wagons destined for the hop kilns of Herefordshire and Worcestershire which served the Midlands. One of the few Welsh breweries to have its own coal wagons was the Felinfoel Brewery at Llangennech, near Llanelli, which were then in the vicinity of Swansea, doubtless to take advantage of local advertising on the wagon side sheets to the breweries main customers, the miners.

Burton beer destined for the docks at Southampton and Portsmouth was carried by the Midland Railway via Tamworth, Birmingham, Worcester and to Cheltenham on its own metals. From Lansdown Junction at Cheltenham the nightly beer trains traversed the GWR Gloucester – Banbury main line to Andoversford Junction. Before 1899 the GWR had controlled rates and charges, but from that year an agreement was made with the Midland & South Western Railway. From Andoversford Junction MSWJR 4–4–0s and 0–6–0s took over, working their ale trains due south via Cirencester, Swindon Town, and Marlborough, all of which also had Great Western stations in addition to those of the MSWJR. South of Marlborough, through the Savernake Forest, the line joined the London & South Western Railway at Red Post Junction on the Salisbury–Basingstoke main line near Andover. From there the goods trains, more usually of mixed freight with their special ale wagons and vans, came under the control of the LSWR. Entire trainloads of beer were often despatched from Burton to be shipped from Southampton Docks of the LSWR, also as victuals for the many passenger ocean liners. From 1914 to 1919, all traffic on this north-south line increased dramatically as a result of the World War I, with entire beer trains arriving at Portsmouth for the

Royal Navy. The LSWR line from Andover Junction continued south via the junction at Fullerton, Stockbridge, Romsey and Redbridge on the western outskirts of Southampton. When the entire trains were going on to Portsmouth Harbour station, the alternative route from Romsey via Eastleigh and Fareham was used.

For a total route mileage of not much more than 160, no fewer than four pre-Grouping main line companies' track was covered, usually accompanied by several locomotive changes from two or more companies. After the grouping, the old MSWJR passed into the hands of the Great Western, which over the next eight years progressively improved and strengthened bridges to allow its own larger locomotives such as the 51xx Class 2–6–2 tanks and the 28xx class of 2–8–0s to use the route. Grange and Manor 4–6–0s were to be seen in abundance, these taking their share of the mixed freights, including their perishable loads of beer. The heavy wartime traffic between 1939 and 1945 repeated the same increased demands of beer for the military at Portsmouth, but with Ministry of Supply austerity and LMS Class 8F 2–8–0 tender locomotives up to 60-wagon loads were handled. The Southern Railway's ubiquitous 2–6–0s did their stint on this cross-country line bringing 'Burton's Best Bitter' to slake the thirst of Southerners. Under British Railways' auspices the final link with the former Midland Railway at Cheltenham was severed on 3 November 1958, finally terminating this beer route which for so long had been the pride of Wiltshire. From the commencement of the Burton beer trade on the MSWJR route on 1 June 1892 as minuted

A farewell chat with the shunter before 'Crab' 2–6–0 No 42763 pulls out of Wetmore sidings at Burton, for its overnight journey south on 26 May 1959. (R. C. Riley)

in the Board of Directors' minutes, some 66 years had elapsed in which beer had 'flowed down the line', leaving Cheltenham in the 7.40am mixed freight.

In June 1882 the General Manager of the Great Eastern Railway reported to the traffic committee that there was a large traffic in yeast from the eastern port of Harwich to the Midlands and the North. He recommended that six purpose-built vans should be provided to run in passenger train formations. These were built that year at Stratford at a cost of £112 each and placed into service. They served their purpose well, as a further six were provided in 1883, although these were rebuilds of earlier open fish trucks. These yeast wagons incorporated louvred sides and ends to the top halves, with the lower sides and ends panelled. These twelve specialised yeast vans were numbered 1801 to 1812 and all were fitted with continuous brakes, enabling them to be used in passenger traffic as required. One of these centenarians has survived in a private garden near the old branch line terminus station at Framlingham, Suffolk, and close inspection reveals that lettering on the waist panel read: 'Yeast Van, GE 1802, Harwich to the North'. The Delft yeast factory was the largest in the country. This yeast traffic to the North eventually finished in 1909/10, no doubt as a result of improved technology in the cultivation of British yeast strains by the Burton brewers. It is all the more surprising that this one remaining yeast van body should have survived some 72 years after it was withdrawn.

The route of this traffic after leaving Harwich was the River Stour valley to Manningtree Junction, thence via Ipswich, Ely and Peterborough, whence it would have been shunted onto trains going to Birmingham and the Midlands via Leicester, or if going further north, via Grantham, Newark, Sheffield and west to Manchester,

another large brewing town. Yeast traffic was also destined for the far north and Scotland, and its journey continued through Leeds, York, Middlesbrough to Newcastle and finally to Edinburgh. Because of the highly perishable nature of yeast it was essential that this traffic was attached to the fastest trains, and where any interchanges were required, smart transfers and connections were made. The design of the yeast vans, incorporating up to 50% louvres, enabled air to circulate within the van, thereby keeping the yeast cool and inactive.

Of all the London goods terminals and depots which received beer from numerous breweries throughout the country, St Pancras claims a unique distinction – it was designed as a module of a beer barrel! This London terminal station was built in the Euston Road for the Midland Railway, designed by the architect Barlow and opened in 1868. The approach lines were built up on brick arches. St Pancras Station is one of the smaller staions, in a very cramped site bounded on three sides by roads, with a major six-road junction under the railway overbridge at the northern end throat. A separate goods depot was situated to the west, but all the beer traffic which came from the Midlands was handled from the centre of the passenger platforms, between Nos 4 and 5. There was a third central track which had a short spur at the northern platform ends, which terminated in a wagon hoist. This delivered single wagons down to ground level which was 20ft below rail level, where cavernous vaults were used for the storage of beer awaiting local delivery. Barlow's design was Gothic, with ironwork built by the Butterley Co, the roof arch girders at 29ft 4in centres giving a roof length of 689ft with a span of 245ft and height of 100ft. There were 700 supporting columns, all spaced on the multiple girth of a beer barrel in order that maximum use should be made of the limited area available. Barlow read a paper to his fellow architects in 1870:

But the station being banded on the south by the Euston Road, on the east by the old St Pancras Road, and on the west by Brewer Street, and the difference in level being such as to admit of the construction of a lower floor with direct access to these streets, the position was deemed so valuable that it was determined by the Directors to devote the whole area to the traffic purposes, communication being made with the rails by means of hydraulic lifts. The special purpose for which this lower floor has been arranged is for Burton beer traffic, and in order to economise the space to the utmost it was determined to use columns and girders instead of brick piers and arches, making the distances between the columns the same as those of the warehouses, which were expressly arranged for the beer traffic. This, in point of fact, the length of a beer barrel became the unit of measure, upon which all the arrangements of this floor were based.

This beer storage and London delivery service was in use up until 1967, when it ceased at the same time as the several Burton breweries' rail closures. Brewers regularly using these facilities were Allsopp, Bass, Benskin, and Ind Coope, which found that the vaults

gave near-ideal controlled temperature conditions. Beneath the busy passenger platforms a hive of activity took place night and day, with the wagon turntables directing wagons onto sidings throughout the entire storage area ready to be off-loaded into horse and motorised drays for morning deliveries.

In 1892 the LSWR purchased Southampton Docks, which as a private company had just lost the valuable Peninsular & Oriental Line passenger traffic to the Great Western Railway at Plymouth. Immediately, dredging began and many other dock improvements commenced, and only a year after the purchase of the docks the famous Inman Line transferred its transatlantic traffic from Liverpool to Southampton. Within five years there were many of the world's most renowned shipping companies operating from Southampton, such as Royal Mail, General Steam Navigation, Rotterdam Lloyd, Union Castle and White Star. With the increasing size of ocean liners new graving docks were built; the Trafalgar Dock completed in 1907 was the world's largest. The White Star line soon had two even larger liners on the stockbooks, the *Olympic* and the *Titanic*, which sailed on her fateful maiden voyage from Southampton in April 1912. The renowned Cunard Line was sailing its flagships *Lusitania* and *Mauretania* to the United States, holding the Blue Riband speed trophy. Victualling stores for this very considerable luxury passenger traffic was carried out by several firms, one of which was the family firm of C. G. Hibbert Ltd, founded in 1767. Its premises were situated in the old central docks area, provided with the LSWR rail sidings into the bottling stores from 1899 to 1940. As with many other parts of the docks, much damage was caused by German bombing in World War II. Liquid refreshment for passengers and crews was provided in bottle and cans by Hibbert, carrying out packaging in its bottling stores. Bulk beer came in rail tankers from Alloa in 'Graham's Golden Lager' privately-owned rail tanks of two and three-dome types, also Allsopp's from Burton-on-Trent. This traffic continued up until 1960 by which time C. G. Hibbert had moved into new premises in the Western Docks, built by the Southern Railway. These docks had been built on marshland infilled with chalk excavated from the large storage sidings area alongside the tunnel at Micheldever on the Waterloo–Winchester main line. Hibbert's premises in the Western Docks were in two sections divided by Solent Road, both having rail sidings, two to the smaller unit on the boundary, with three sidings, including one into a building, on the larger central complex. Beside these bottling stores a fan of 18 storage sidings served the remainder of the modern docks. Bottling at Hibbert's new bonded stores ceased in 1975, although canning continues to this day, supplied by bulk road tankers from the same locations as in the days of the considerable rail traffic. In the post-war years, Whitbread made use of Dyson-built road trailers, similar to those in use by Arthur Guinness & Son. These twin glass-lined road/rail tanks took Whitbread

Deeley 0–4–0 side tank No 41536 shunts beer vans on the main line beside maltings at Shobnall, Burton-on-Trent. (*R. C. Riley*)

beers to Belgium, where its agencies were very strong. The return journey via Hibbert's at Southampton brought back Oranjeboom Lager, becoming increasingly popular as one of the several continental lagers which Londoners enjoy. This joint road/rail traffic ceased when Breda/Oranjeboom became part of the Allied Breweries European interests in the 1970s.

Immediately on taking over the Southampton Docks, William Adams, the LSWR locomotive superintendent at Nine Elms, designed the short wheelbase Class B4 0–4–0T specifically for the docks traffic. Fourteen of these delightful locomotives were built, all bearing continental names. The last was withdrawn in 1963, and is preserved to remind us of its pleasant duty of shunting beer around the large dock network. There were also the two Class C14 0–4–0T which like the B4s were ousted by USA 0–6–0 tanks purchased after the war. Present-day passenger traffic is now but a shadow of its former self, with the Ocean Liner Terminal handling the Cunard Line's *Queen Elizabeth 2*, still requiring liquid refreshment, but alas not now transported by railways.

The London & South Western Railway was greatly concerned after complaints by passengers of poor standards in several of their station refreshment rooms. These facilities were leased to tenants, and in June 1882 a contract for all refreshment rooms was given to one firm, Simmonds, taken-over in June 1888 by Spier & Pond in order to improve matters. The LSWR recorded on 26 April 1882 its 'opinion that it is essential in the interests of the travelling public that Messrs Bass' and Allsopp's beers should be supplied at all refreshment rooms'. Happily a wide range of beers is still available at the larger BR stations, with canned beers on the restaurant and buffet cars on major long-distance

routes. In 1948 the Southern Region introduced a new 'tavern car' on the Atlantic Coast Express. This was a standard Bulleid coach decorated like the olde worlde English public house, both inside and out, with painted brick-work dado, wall rendering and mock beams. On the bar counter top, draught Ind Coope and Allsopp's bitter was served straight from the wood, with the then new keg beer, Double Diamond, as stable mate. Bottled beers, wines, spirits and minerals were also served, but unfortunately this experiment did not prove successful and only lasted a few years.

The hop pickers

Paddock Wood is the centre of the 'hop country', situated in the Weald of Kent, on the old South Eastern Railway main line between Tonbridge and the railway town of Ashford. Today the Hop College and research centre is at Paddock Wood, which was once the junction for Hawkhurst, some 11½ miles south-east, set in delightful countryside dotted with the distinctive oast houses in hop gardens and fruit orchards.

The Hawkhurst branch line is remembered by many thousands of hop-pickers who came from the working-class areas of London to the Kentish hop gardens to spend a three-week working holiday gathering the crop. Entire families lived in spartan huts provided by the farmers, working long days stripping the hop-vines from the tall wires and placing the hop cones in 6ft sacks called 'pockets'. By night hoards of pickers would descend on the local village pubs to quench their thirst, causing many a melee with the locals, with whom they were not popular.

The Hawkhurst Branch was built in 1892, and appropriately the ceremonial first train, pulled by a Cudworth E Class 2–4–0, was garlanded in hop vines, October being the height of the picking season. The line's engineer was Colonel Stephens, who gave his engineering and management skills to the branch line until his death in 1931. The line had several steep gradients, 1 in 66 to 1 in 78, and two short tunnels, the gradients often causing problems to the heavily-laden hop pickers' specials. Regular motive power after World War I was the R and R1 classes 0–4–4 tanks of the South Eastern & Chatham Railway. Wainwright H 0–4–4Ts and C Class 0–6–0s shedded at Tonbridge were rostered for passenger duties. Stirling O Class 0–6–0s regularly pulled the freight trains, while his B Class 4–4–0 tender engines worked on passenger trains in the 1920s. Right to the end the hop-pickers trains were formed of SECR birdcage sets normally reserved for excursion use.

To transport large numbers of hop-pickers special trains were provided, chiefly from London Bridge Station. Paddock Wood provided a co-ordination 'hop control centre'. Regular hop-picking families were notified by special postcards sent by the farmers advising train, date, time and destination. In 1912 there were 26 hop-pickers' specials carrying approximately 350 on each train. By 1952 there were 56 specials, carrying 4,500 pickers, whose ranks were swollen by some 23,000 friends at weekends. Seven years later the rail traffic had slumped to one two-coach train on a Sunday with a return through working to London Bridge. Previously up to eleven passenger trains arrived in London within a four-hour period, with two off the Hawkhurst Branch, three from the main line at Sevenoaks, and a further four from the Maidstone area.

Freight traffic coming inwards to many country goods yards for use in the hop industry included woollen waste, called 'shoddy', which was either loose or in sacks stacked tightly in vans. This material is used as a fertilizer and came from the woollen mill areas, 'with Bradford and Kidderminster being the chief despatch points. The 'shoddy' was handled by specialist agents who collected the material from the mills, it being high in ammonia and nitrogen, ideal fertilizers for the hops. The wool waste was spread around the hop 'hills' at the rate of 1 to 2 tons per acre, and on average every three years. The outward traffic consisting of the very large but lightweight hop pockets, was loaded up at several stations. The type of open wagon used in earlier days was the SECR half-round high-ended tarpaulin, these being later replaced by standard closed 10-ton and 12-ton vans.

Second to the Weald of Kent as a hop-producing area is Hereford and Worcester. Ledbury, on the delightful foothills of the Malvern Hills, is the administrative centre for this Midlands hop area, which so conveniently serves the great breweries in Birmingham to the North, and further on those at Burton-on-Trent and Manchester. The Great Western Railway enjoyed much hop traffic to these destinations, also to smaller stations on its system, such as Stratford-on-Avon some 30 miles due east, The South Wales, Bristol and Gloucester breweries were well served by the GWR for hops from Worcestershire and malt from maltings eventually owned by the Associated British Maltsters group at Wallingford, Abingdon and Bath, all served by their own private rail sidings. Each of these

maltings regularly dispatched malt in 20-ton grain hopper vans, finally ceasing to do so in the 1960s when the inevitable road transport replaced British Railways' local freight traffic.

Of still lesser importance as a hop centre is Alton in Hampshire. When the Mid-Hants line opened on 20 October 1865 a siding was provided into the Alton Brewery, with a turntable giving a spur siding crossing over Windmill Hill Road which divided the brewery. Hop kilns were prolific around the brewery and took advantage of the railway to transport their products to the London markets. A nightly train left the Alton Brewery with beer for the Nine Elms goods depot of the LSWR, with the occasional covered van full of hop pockets.

Kentish brewers with their own private-livery vans included Shepherd Neame & Co of Faversham, which not only had several beer stores in Kent and Sussex but also at New Cross and Bromley, serving the developing south-eastern outskirts of London. At least three wagons were in use as early as 1867, each with a load of eight tons; these were built by the Gloucester Railway Carriage & Wagon Co. Ltd. They were replaced by several built by R. Y. Pickering of Wishaw in 1912, with a modified livery which gave half of the signwriting to the 'London Stores, Camberwell and Penge'. These remained in use bringing their cargoes of 'Faversham Ales' to South London well into the 1920s. At Maidstone Fremlin Bros, also transported its ales on the South Eastern & Chatham Railway from before 1900, not only to its Buckingham Palace Road store in London, but also to Brighton and Rochester, travelling on a regular weekly basis over the metals of the London, Brighton & South Coast Railway.

GREAT EASTERN RAILWAY

Goods Manager's Office,
　　Liverpool Street Station,
　　　　London, E.C., 1st October, 1880.

Brewers' and Distillers' Grains

Scale of Rates for the conveyance of the above traffic, in truck loads of 5 tons and upwards, at the Owner's Risk, Station to Station, and exclusive of loading and unloading between Country Stations (with a few exceptions), distant 50 miles or more apart, on the Great Eastern Railway:–

	Per ton.	
	s.	d.
Up to 50 miles	4	2
51 to 60 „	4	7
61 to 70 „	5	0
71 to 85 „	5	5
86 to 100 „	5	10
101 to 120 „	6	3
121 and above	6	8

W. GARDNER,
Goods Manager.

3

Burton, a town of breweries and railways

Four pre-grouping main line railway companies served the town of Burton-on-Trent. The first to arrive was the Birmingham & Derby Junction Railway which came to the town in 1839, and became in 1844 the famous 'Midland', distinguished by its attractive crimson lake livery. In 1848 the North Staffordshire Railway entered Burton from the north via Tutbury and its junction, linking the brewing town with Derby and Crewe. On 28 January 1878 the Great Northern Railway came to Burton and was operating goods traffic from that date, with passenger services via Egginton Junction from 1 July. The fourth company, the London & North Western Railway had running powers over the Midland Railway lines via Wychnor Junction to the south-west of the town from 1849.

The present passenger station is situated a few hundred yards to the west of the original station, which was built to serve the North Staffordshire Railway and the Great Northern Railway on the north side platforms

Midland Railway passenger station looking towards Birmingham, with a freight train loaded up with beer casks awaiting delivery into Ind Coope's premises on the left. (*R. C. Riley collection*)

and LNWR on the south. The main through lines of the Midland Railway were served by an island platform, with local Midland Railway branch line services jointly sharing the southern platform with the LNWR. The road access to the station was by Station Street which also served the adjacent Samuel Allsopp brewery. This road originally crossed the main line on the level, with crossing gates that caused numerous delays, so by 1883 a road overbridge was built in conjunction with new station buildings. The approach road curved to the west from opposite the brewery entrance, with the old 'straight' stretch of Station Street still visible today. A small pull-in forecourt was provided for the setting-down and collection of passengers to the high-level station precincts. Broad flights of steps led down to the island platforms, with their glass canopies supported on intricate cast-iron spandrels.

At the grouping of the railway companies in 1923, the four companies lines serving Burton-on-Trent became part of the London, Midland & Scottish Railway; when British Railways was formed on 1 January 1948 the area came under the London Midland Region, controlled from Derby.

All the branch lines built in the town, primarily to

serve the breweries, were constructed by the Midland Railway. The LNWR had running powers over most lengths, granted at various times. This company also acted on behalf of the NSR. Several Acts of Parliament were passed, authorising the construction of the branch lines and sidings passing over the public highways. The Midland Railway and 'Bass' were granted permission under the Burton-on-Trent Railways Acts of 1859, 1860, 1865, 1867, 1878 and 1881. The LNW Railways Act of 1861, The Great Northern Railway Act of 1874, and the North Staffordshire Railway Act 1863, also gave the necessary authority.

At the turn of the century there were 32 level-crossings in Burton, with Station Street being crossed three times and Guild Street, Horninglow Street, New Street, Park Street and Lichfield Street all being crossed twice. Notices proclaiming 'Caution!', 'These gates will be opened when the bell Rings', were warnings to pedestrians that the level-crossing gates were about to 'close', as the signs referred to their opening for the brewery rail traffic! The bells heralded the approach of one of the smart brewery locomotives, most likely the unusual 'Turkey red' of the Bass fleet, possibly inspired by the Midlands crimson lake; others would be in the olive green of the Ind Coope & Allsopp fleet or the royal blue and scarlet of the Worthington locomotives. Most of these sported polished copper and brass to which the crews were justly proud. As the gates closed, so the locomotive pulled slowly across with its load of up to fifteen wagons. In early times several of these would have been the elaborately painted privately-owned wagons, with their wholesome bold lettering. Later in the British Railways era, most of the vans and open trucks were of the shock-absorbing type, with their distinctive three white bands on sides and ends.

There were six 'main' branch lines, named after the streets to which they most closely related – Guild Street, High Street, Horninglow, Shobnall, Hay, and Bond End. Two lesser branches were the Dallow Lane and Allsopp's Cooperage, the former owned by the LNWR, the latter by Samuel Allsopp & Sons. To accommodate the considerable transfer of wagons to the numerous breweries, to assemble the 'beer trains', and to store up to several hundred empty wagons for emergency traffic requirements, large marshalling yards were constructed. To the south-west of Burton on the Birmingham side of town were the Branston Sidings. These were located near the triangular Branston/Leicester Junctions and also the Midland Railway locomotive depot. To the north-east side of town, there were the Dixie Sidings, between the Hay and Guild Street branches, and opposite the Dallow Lane Branch which turned due north. Further to the east were situated the Whetmore Sidings, on the south side of the main line. Immediately to the south was the Horninglow Street Goods Yard and the LNWR locomotive shed, where also the GNR traffic was handled.

Goods and mineral trains were required to run on the goods lines between Leicester Junction and Whetmore sidings, although when carrying out this transfer it was not necessary to include a brake van. The following notes were taken from the Midland Railway Working Timetable Appendix of 1911:

Guild Street Branch
The up line of the Guild Street Branch between the Hay Branch and High Street Crossing is worked as a single line by Train Staff, without tickets. The Train Staff must be carried by each train or engine running between the Hay Branch and High Street Crossing, and no train or engine must be on the single line between those points without the Train Staff. High Street Crossing Signalbox is the Train Staff station, and the Signalman on duty is the sole person authorised to deliver or receive same.

When a train or engine, the Driver of which is not in possession of the Train Staff, required to run on the single line from the Hay Branch to High Street Crossing and the Guard or Shunter must proceed to High Street Crossing and obtain the Staff from the Signalman on duty there and then return to the Hay Branch and hand the Staff to the driver.

When a train or engine requires to run on the single line from High Street Crossing to the Hay Branch, and does not require to return to High Street Crossing, the Driver must obtain the Staff from the Signalman and retain it in his possession until he has run clear of the Guild Street Branch on to the Hay Branch, and when this has been done he must hand the Staff to the Guard or Shunter, who must at once return it to the Signalman at High Street Crossing.

Engine drivers must be extremely careful not to take the Staff beyond High Street Crossing when proceeding from the direction of the Hay Branch, and, except when requiring to return to High Street Crossing must be careful to deliver it up in accordance with instructions on reaching the Hay Branch.

Hawkins Lane Junction
G.N. goods trains running from the Midland Railway to the G.N.R. at Hawkins Lane Junction, must not exceed 35 wagons, and G.N. goods trains running from G.N.R. to Midland Railway via Hawkins Lane Junction must not exceed 20 wagons.

Branch to Bass & Co's Shobnall Maltings
The line of rails farthest from Messrs Bass & Co's maltings on the Midland main line side of the maltings between Wellington Street Junction and Shobnall Maltings Signalbox, is worked by Train Tablet in accordance with the Regulations for Train Signalling on Single Lines or Railway worked on the Electric Train Tablet Block System. The Wellington Street Junction and Shobnall Maltings Signalboxes are the Train Tablet Stations.

The points in the single running line on the Wellington Street Junction side of Shobnall Maltings Signalbox are worked by Guards and Shunters from a stage, and controlled by Train Tablet in accordance with Rule 34 of Electric Train Tablet Block Regulations.

All wagons from Leicester Junction to Shobnall Maltings sidings must be taken in front of the engine. A Guards brake in which a Guard must ride, must be taken in front of the wagons. Not more than 30 wagons at any one time.

Dallow Lane Wharf
All Midland Railway trains and engines going to Dallow Lane Wharf must stop at the Signalbox at Allsopp's siding,

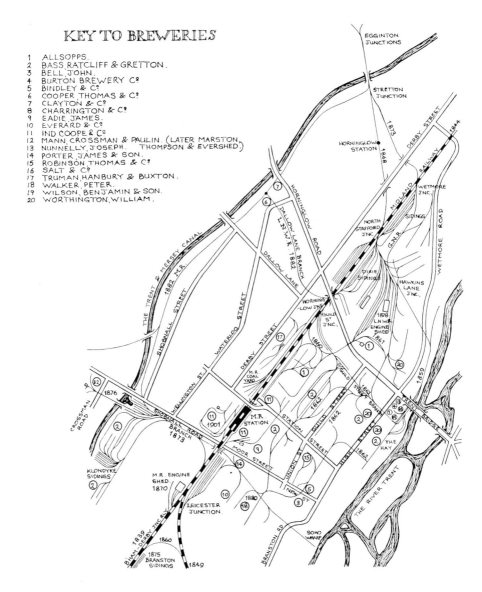

KEY TO BREWERIES

1. ALLSOPPS.
2. BASS, RATCLIFF & GRETTON.
3. BELL, JOHN.
4. BURTON BREWERY Cº
5. BINDLEY & Cº
6. COOPER, THOMAS & Cº
7. CLAYTON & Cº
8. CHARRINGTON & Cº
9. EADIE, JAMES.
10. EVERARD & Cº
11. IND COOPE & Cº
12. MANN, CROSSMAN & PAULIN. (LATER MARSTON,
13. NUNNELLY, JOSEPH.   THOMPSON & EVERSHED.)
14. PORTER, JAMES & SON.
15. ROBINSON, THOMAS & Cº
16. SALT & Cº
17. TRUMAN, HANBURY & BUXTON.
18. WALKER, PETER.
19. WILSON, BENJAMIN & SON.
20. WORTHINGTON, WILLIAM.

Burton-on-Trent's brewery railway network at the turn of the century, with dates indicating the growth of the branch lines. (*M. Steele/Author*)

and the Signalman will accompany them to the Wharf, to work the signals for the protection of such trains and engines.

Shobnall & Bond End, Burton

Loads for small tank engines of 1500 class will be 25 loaded and 37 empties and for shunting engines of 1601 class, 35 loaded and 50 empties.

Most level-crossings were controlled by signalboxes up to the full standards and appearance of the main line railway companies. These were operated by main line staff, who used the usual bell system for the acceptance of trains, and also operated strictly to the railway company regulations. Whistle codes were used by the

locomotive crews to indicate their intentions to the signalbox man. Shunters always accompanied each train, sometimes several could be seen in the open cabs or hanging on to the wagons, with their shunting poles safely rested. There were several crossings which did not have signalboxes, but exposed ground frames at which a man was required to be constantly on duty. As with main line practice, these road crossing were also signalled. Two types of signal were in evidence right up to closure – ordinary semaphore arms, mounted on either wood or concrete posts, (the latter sometimes open slotted, were most numerous) and in one or two locations they stood cheek-by-jowl with ancient revolving crossbar arms, a strange sight indeed to modern eyes.

Locomotives to handle the Midland Railway Company goods traffic were allocated to the Burton locomotive shed. Standard Midland 6-wheel tender locomotives, with outside springs and Salter safety-valves were the mainstay for freight trains going to areas of the Midland system. For the local shunting duties and running on the branch lines, 6-wheel well-tanks were used, again with outside springs and scant protection for the crews. Several of this very early type, built in 1855, were still working in 1920. Later the tender engines were superseded by American-built 2–6–0s; these locomotives were distinctive with their unusual dome-shaped and commodious cabs. The Edwardian engine drivers like their earlier Victorian predecessors were proud and respected men. There was a hierarchy amongst them, the top-flight passenger express drivers at the top, the local shunters at the bottom; below the drivers were the firemen with their own scale, and then the cleaners, yard men, and many other trades at the locomotive depots. During the 1960s under British Railways auspices there were fifteen Fowler 2–6–0s shedded at Burton, whose duties included some passenger work. There were also 25 Class 4F and five Class 3F 0–6–0s, the latter rostered for local and shunting duties. Even up to the early 1960s Midland Railway locomotives of Classes 2F, 3F and 4F were still in use. Early in 1959, shunting duties of the old steam locomotives were gradually being replaced by 350hp diesel shunters which worked at the three main marshalling yards. The Shobnall and Bond End branches at this time were still being shunted by the unusual Midland Railway Deeley 0–4–0 tanks, with their tanks extending to the front of the smokebox. Nos 41532 and 41536 of this class worked these branches because of the several tight curves encountered. Other tank shunting duties were carried out by four of Class 3F 0–6–0s. Many of the St Pancras beer trains were allocated to Fowler 'Crab' 2–6–0s, hauling 30 to 40 wagons. On occasions LNER K3 Moguls were to be seen on this roster, usually setting off from Burton around 6.15pm. The LNWR locomotives most commonly used were the Webb

'Cauliflower' 0–6–0s in black livery. By the early 1960s, all these beer trains were fully fitted, allowing good speeds to be achieved. Even around the turn of the century, when several breweries had their own privately-owned ventilated vans, these were fitted with vacuum brakes so that they could be used in fast traffic workings.

During the last decade of the beer traffic handled by British Railways this was carried out much as it was in the early 1920s by the pre-grouping companies. Most through freight trains which called at Burton to either set down or pick-up wagons, called at the Whetmore sidings. This was also the starting point for most of the northbound trains, while those going south started across the main line at Horninglow Bridge Yard. The more important beer trains which originated entirely at Burton are tabulated separately.

In the post-war period when British Rail started to examine more closely its operating costs, particularly of manpower, it became evident that charges to breweries would have to be increased. At any given time there were as many as 1,000 wagons being used for ale traffic but at no charge to the breweries. British Rail pressed for higher freight charges, in turn the breweries examined their own costs of transportation.

The railway strike by ASLEF footplatemen from 29 May to 15 June 1955 highlighted the precarious position of several of the larger breweries, when at very short notice they had to make alternative arrangements for the transport of their beer and for the inward raw materials. Because of the near-total dependence on the railway transport by Bass, that company was the most vulnerable. Firstly, to combat the increased demurrage charges of British Rail, Mr Len Hayward, Bass transport manager, purchased 150 wagons and vans for £7,200 and these remained in use until 1967, the time of the Bass rail closure. The equivalent charges over the same period by British Rail would have been in the region of £140,000 for the use of wagons.

A further threat in 1958 to stop all rail transit, this

PRINCIPAL FREIGHT TRAINS FROM BURTON-ON-TRENT, MID-1960s

Departure	Days	Class	Destination	Conveying traffic for
4.00pm	SO	D	St Pancras	London
4.20pm	SX	C	Bristol	Cheltenham, Gloucester, Bristol
6.15pm	SX	C	York	York and beyond
6.50pm	SX	C	St Pancras	London
6.55pm	SX	E	Colwick	Manchester, Hull, Boston, Doncaster
7.55pm	SX	D	Rowsley (1)	Rowsley, Manchester
8.25pm	SX	C	Carlisle	Heysham, Barrow, Carnforth, Lancaster and Scotland
8.45pm	SX	E	Crewe	Macclesfield, Chester and North Wales
9.10pm	MO	C	Niddrie	Scottish East Coast
9.30pm	SX	D	Swansea	Brecon, Wellington, Shrewsbury and South Wales
9.33pm		E	Nuneaton (2)	Nuneaton, Rugby, Leamington, Bletchley
10.40pm		C	Nottingham (3)	Nottingham, Lincoln
11.10pm	SX	D	Wigston	London, Leicester, the Eastern Counties, via Peterborough
10.54pm		C	Leeds (4)	North Eastern Region
2.00am	MX	E	Sheffield (5)	Chesterfield, Sheffield
2.53am	MX	D	Derby (6)	Derby

Trains started at Burton-on-Trent with the following exceptions:–

(1)	5.10pm	Birmingham	(3)	9.15pm	Water Orton	(5)	11.30pm	Birmingham
(2)	7.48pm	Nottingham	(4)	9.55pm	Birmingham	(6)	6.20pm	Bristol

Busy scene at Wetmore sidings in 1959 with a beer train being assembled in the foreground, and a Class 3F 0–6–0 waiting for the right of way in the background. (*R. C. Riley*)

time by the National Union of Railwaymen at the Whit-Monday, had Bass feverishly making provision for road transport to enter its premises. Nothing was more symbolic than the demolition on 9 May 1958 of the central pillars at the main entrance gates (built of masonry quoins and brick panels way back in the 1870s) to allow access to the large articulated tankers, nicknamed 'Sputniks'. British Rail was now faced with large volumes of its freight traffic being lost to the roads, and so it opened discussions with several of the breweries with the view to providing bulk freight containers. A proposed depot at Burton however was not approved, due to the scarcity of capital for investment – that which was available was put into large depots at railheads. By 1967, both Marston and Bass had completely abandoned their rail systems. Ind Coope alone retained a few sidings for the receipt of grain vans, this traffic still being in existence, albeit of a very light nature, into the 1980s.

In the same year as the termination of rail ale, the level-crossing gates were removed, with the exception of the ones at Park Street, which were removed ten years later in 1977. The overall effect on the rail traffic at Burton of the loss of its previous brewery traffic was traumatic. For the railway enthusiast it was the loss of a colourful and fascinating industrial railway network; to the Burtonian it was the loss of 100 years of history in his town, the lifeblood of his livelihood – 'Burton, Beer and Buffers'.

British Rail soon transferred its sundries traffic to Derby, followed by the parcels traffic. The large bonded stores to the east of Burton, along with the warehousing business, was transferred to the newly-created National Freight Corporation, needless to say a road venture. The branch lines and sidings were soon removed leaving a few, such as those into the Ind Coope Brewery, also several at Shobnall. The large single-span girder bridge over the Trent & Mersey Canal, which was the extension from the Shobnall Branch into the Marston Brewery remains intact, as do several sidings and the locomotive shed within the brewery. Likewise the Ind Coope engine shed off Moor Street remains in use as a store. After the rail traffic ceased, the sad and melancholy mood prevailed for many months, with Bass vans and wagons being collected together and eventually broken up, along with several locomotives. One or two locomotives survived the carnage and are preserved, keeping our memories alive of the happy days when their steam and oil smells mixed so happily with the brewing smells of Burton. Never again will we be able to revel in these nostalgic sights, sounds and smells. Alas, an end to a glorious era.

4

Samuel Allsopp & Son Ltd, Station and High Street, Burton

The year 1708 was an important one in the annals of English history, when Marlborough had a resounding success on the Continent, defeating Louis XIV. Queen Anne was on the throne and there was much political unrest. In these uncertain circumstances, Burton's first brewer commenced his trade – one Benjamin Wilson, Esq. His daugher married James Allsopp in 1777, and their son, Samuel, gave his name to the firm until its amalgamation with Ind Coope & Co in 1934.

Wilson's brewery was situated in the High Street, close to the Hay and the River Trent, where over the years several other brewers also built their breweries. Transport of his beer was down the river as far as Gainsborough and Hull, where it was loaded onto large sailing ships which traded with the Baltic ports. This export trade lasted for many years and was the backbone to his business. With fluctuating trade abroad caused by political unrest in Russia and France, when Thomas Allsopp was doing his utmost to sell his products, he embarked on a 'home' sales promotion around 1820. While on a visit to London in 1822 he met a director of the East India Company, and their conversation turned to the trading difficulties that Allsopp was encountering. He suggested that Allsopp turn his attention to the warmer climates, such as the Indian market, and thereupon produced a bottle of beer which he had brought back from India. Allsopp immediately accepted the challenge to produce a similar beer, and consulting his veteran maltster, Job Goodhead, they produced the first Burton India Pale Ale in a teapot!

Business expanded by leaps and bounds, so much so that when a cask census was made in 1854, Allsopp had 100,000, the business still being carried out on Wilson's original site on the banks of the Trent. The firm's prosperity now justified further expansion which this site did not allow, and so the 'New Brewery' was built alongside the Midland Railway main line in 1860. The new brewery covered 50 acres and was the largest brewery on one site in this country, a marvel in its day.

Allsopp & Sons Ltd locally-built Thornwill & Warham No 4, built in 1847 and scrapped in 1926. (*Courtesy F. Jones*)

Hudswell, Clarke & Rogers Works No 168 built in 1875 for Samuel Allsopp & Sons, No 4 in the brewery fleet. The open cab afforded scant protection for its crew. (*F. Jones collection*)

It was at this time that the whimsical Charles Stuart Calverley wrote these lines:

He what should shine, and petrify his tutor,
Should drink draught Allsopp in its native pewter.

Because of the proximity to the main railway line and passenger station, ale loading soon commenced at the new brewery. Allsopp had built up an agency and depot sales and distribution system, with services from Burton either direct to customers' premises on a delivered and cellared basis or from company depots, many of them with similar private sidings facilities and traffic on a private siding to private siding basis. In the former the railway companies were contracted to provide a through service, including the collection of empty casks. Company depots at this time amounted to 15, with the entire London operation being handled at St Pancras Station. Here was situated a wagon lift at the north end of the station, which lowered a full wagon down to street level for unloading into the cellars beneath the station arches. Extensive use was made of railheads for beer distribution in casks, such as No 1 Coal Road, Leeds Midland, Crewe Coal Yard, East Gate Sidings, Hythe, but in particular Leicester Fish Dock Road NE and Leicester Midland. There was great competition for this traffic and the two local goods agents 'waited upon' the brewery traffic manager each Monday morning to obtain his business for that week!

The Leicester fish dock traffic was sent from the brewery via the Horninglow Street crossing, thence via the NE routes – Horninglow, Egginton Junction, Derby Friargate, Ilkeston thence to Leicester. The Midland Railway traffic was by the more direct route, and presumably cheaper, via Leicester Junction, Gresley, Ashby, and Coalville.

At Shobnall, new maltings were built and connected to the railway network and opened for the receipt of grain vans from 27 October 1880. A contractor's locomotive was in use for this shunting to the Midland Railway junction. The first sidings into the brewery were worked by horses from the Guild Street branch as from 4 October 1862 until February 1865. From this date engines began working down the Hay. A branch to Allsopp's cooperage, situated on the east side of Horninglow Street, which crossed at right-angles over the Guild Street branch, was opened in November 1861. This was known as 'Allsopp's Crossing', with a signalbox controlling the potentially dangerous intersection. From 13 November 1882 the GNR ceased to hand-over Allsopp's traffic from the Shobnall maltings and the LNWR Dallow Lane Wharf to the Midland Railway for conveyance by Midland locomotive to those points, but handed this traffic directly to the LNWR locomotives.

John Morris & Son, Coopers, of Horninglow Street purchased some premises at Church Croft from Allsopp, and made use of Allsopp's sidings facilities for their cask staves from 16 November 1903, in which Allsopp locomotives brought in loaded wagons. At this time, S. Allsopp & Son paid to the Midland Railway the

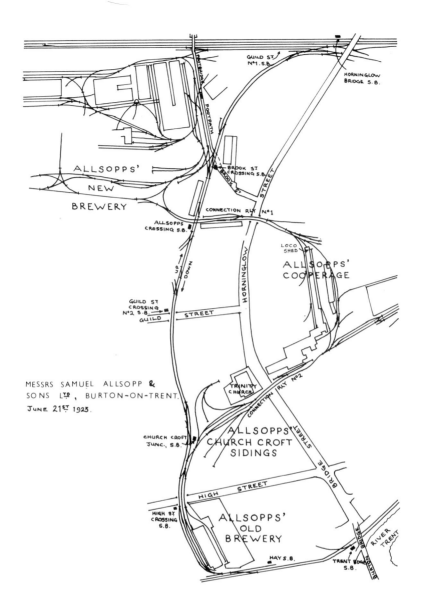

GUILD ST
N°1 S.B.

HORNINGLOW
BRIDGE S.B.

ALLSOPPS'
NEW
BREWERY

BROOK ST
CROSSING S.B.

CONNECTION RLY N°1

ALLSOPPS
CROSSING S.B.

LOCO
SHED

ALLSOPPS'
COOPERAGE

GUILD ST
CROSSING
N°2 S.B.
GUILD STREET

HORNINGLOW

S DOWN

MESSRS SAMUEL ALLSOPP &
SONS LTD, BURTON-ON-TRENT.
JUNE 21ST 1923.

CONNECTION RLY N°2

TRINITY
CHURCH

CHURCH CROFT
JUNC. S.B.

ALLSOPPS'
CHURCH CROFT
SIDINGS

STREET

BRIDGE

HIGH STREET

HIGH ST
CROSSING
S.B.

ALLSOPPS'
OLD
BREWERY

HAY S.B.

BROOK HORNINGLOW

TRENT BDGE
S.B.

RIVER
TRENT

sum of £40 per annum for running powers over the Hay and Guild Street branches.

Allsopp's provided a two-road engine shed at the cooperage just across Horninglow Road, backing onto and connecting to the LNWR goods yard. The total mileage of sidings amounted to ten, laid out in an 'S' shape, with the Old Brewery at the Southern end of the town, while in the middle curve was Allsopp's cooperage, with the New Brewery in the Northern tip.

Allsopp had several privately-owned covered vans, painted in the brash Victorian style; this consisted of a creamy-yellow bodywork with white roof and black ironwork, except white-walled wheels. Bold block lettering was in black with red shading, with company name and 'Lager Beer'. The company's trade mark of the 'Red Hand' was sited twice in the centre. These vans

Allsopp's complex layout in its heyday, connecting the 'Old Brewery' down by the River Trent with the cooperage and locomotive shed in the centre, and the 'New Brewery' alongside the Midland main line. (*Ind Coope, Burton Brewery Co*)

were 8 ton capacity, ventilated and fitted with vacuum brakes, enabling them to be used in fast traffic workings. Many years later, when Allsopp amalgamated with Ind Coope (in the true sense of the word – Ind Coope & Allsopp), tank wagons of 11 tons were used for bulk lager traffic. These rail tank wagons were built by Charles Roberts & Co Ltd of Wakefield, from around 1938. Several designs were in use, and the livery varied from all black with no lettering, to white with black lettering. Each tank wagon number was

Morning assembly outside the old Allsopp locomotive shed in 1957, with the English Electric No 9 in front of Sentinel No 7 and two locally-built Baguley diesels. (R. C. Riley)

painted on each barrel end in large numerals. The capacity of these tankers was 2,160 gallons.

The first locomotive delivered to Allsopp was the locally-made Thornewill & Warham 0–4–0 well tank, in 1863. This had 14in x 20in cylinders, and as originally built was without any weather protection for the locomotive crew. Later it was rebuilt with enclosed cab (except to the rear) and with a saddle tank, complete with handsome brass salter valve dome. Outside valve gear was an unusual feature, as was the filled-in step to the front of the footplate. During the next ten years, Hudswell Clarke & Rodgers supplied two 4-wheel saddle tanks, also without cabs. These were works numbers 146 of 1874 and 168 of 1875. Even at this early time, the locomotives sported very handsome brass oval company name plates with a raised 'hand' motif in the centre. The livery was mid-green relieved with a broad black band and a fine orange line on either side. Many years later, in 1925, the fourth Allsopp locomotive was supplied by Andrew Barclay. A Scottish manufacturer was no doubt chosen because of

the predilection of the managing director, John H Calder, a Scot, who held this appointment from 1912.

In 1949, T. W. Ward of Sheffield re-laid much of the track, replacing cobblestones by concrete, as it was a daily occurrence for the locomotives to become derailed, with the sharp curves and many years of wartime neglect. It was quite a sight to see the Bagnall or Hawthorn 'on a skew' with safety valves blowing-off and the engineers and platelayers working furiously with jacks and packing pieces to re-rail the locomotive, with a crowd of onlookers cheering them on!

The Romford firm of Ind Coope & Co built a brewery alongside the Allsopp New Brewery in 1858. It had been a matter of much speculation for many years as to when these two side-by-side breweries would amalgamate. In the early part of 1934 rumours were rife, and it came as no great surprise when in April of that year the directors of both companies published the announcement. The symbolic knocking-down of a dividing wall of the two neighbours was the herald of the new company – Ind, Coope & Allsopp Ltd. On 1 January 1959, 'Allsopp' was dropped from the title, as it was considered no longer appropriate. The name of Allsopp does however still live on in distant parts, as 'Allsopp Lager' is canned and exported to Africa.

5

Bass, Ratcliffe and Gretton, High Street, Burton

William Bass had a successful general cartage business operating out of Burton, often carrying small brewers' products to the river and canal for onward transit. With his contact of several brewers he was eventually able to invest some of his profits into a small brewery of his own. His elder son, Michael, born in 1759, inherited the business, and his skills as a brewer and salesman were such that at his death in 1827, his brewery was the most important of its time in Burton. His son, Michael Thomas Bass became a prominent notary in the town, becoming a Member of Parliament in 1848, representing Derby for 35 years. His abiding interest was in the elevation of the working classes, and in particular with the railwaymen of Derby. His action in representing the railwaymen in Parliament brought pressure to bear on the Midland Railway and he was instrumental in their improved working conditions. Not only was his benefaction towards his constituents but also to his brewery employees, as he instituted a library, social and health service, sporting and banking facilities. He also gave large sums of money for the construction of St Paul's Church, an infirmary, children's hospital and railway orphanage.

The construction of the Midland Railway main line from Derby during the 1830s gave a considerable fillip to the brewing industry, allowing the speedy transit of its beer to much greater customer catchment areas. To make use of the railways, the beer had to get to the railway goods yards. Two-wheeled horse-drawn drays, known as 'floaters', were used; these were low-slung for ease of loading the heavy casks, the maximum load capable of being drawn by the heavy horses being one ton. Congestion in the town of Burton soon became rampant, with continuous streams of floaters making their way between the scattered breweries throughout the town.

Between 1860 and 1880, several Acts of Parliament were passed to enable the construction of connecting branch lines and sidings throughout the town, linking many of the breweries with the main line. By the end of the century there were some 40 miles of private railway, of which Bass had running powers over 26 miles in all. The entreprenurial breweries, and Bass was certainly one, soon took advantage of other brewers' malaise, and so the absorbtion of the breweries less able to weather the storms in difficult times saw the growth of the fittest. So it was that many scattered breweries throughout the town became absorbed into the Bass

empire. By 1900 there were 21 breweries but 11 years later this had been reduced to 17. Among the larger breweries to be absorbed into Bass at this time was Thomas Salt & Co Ltd. Many years before this arrangement in 1906, Messrs William Gratton of New Street, and Samuel Ratcliffe of High Street had joined with the Bass family.

The Bass private railway system came into use in 1862; on 4 October inward traffic, consisting of malt and coal was received, with the first outward consignment of beer leaving on 7 November. This

ANNO VICESIMO OCTAVO & VICESIMO NONO

VICTORIÆ REGINÆ.

****

Cap. ccxliii.

An Act to authorize the Construction of a Railway in the Town of *Burton-upon-Trent;* and for other Purposes. [5th *July* 1865.]

WHEREAS by " The *Midland* Railway and *Burton-upon-Trent* Bridge Act, 1859," and " The *Midland* Railway (*Burton* Branches) Act, 1860," the *Midland* Railway Company were empowered to construct within the Town of *Burton-upon-Trent* the Railways in those respective Acts mentioned, one of which Railways was authorized to be constructed across and on the Level of a Street in the said Town called *Guild Street,* and another of which Railways was authorized to be constructed across and on the Level of a Street in the said Town called *High Street:* And whereas the said Railways have for some Time past been completed and opened for Traffic, and by reason thereof a great Diminution in the Passage of Traffic along the Streets of the said Town has been effected, and Obstructions to the Passage of Traffic have decreased, and further Convenience to the Inhabitants of and others frequenting the said Town would result from the Construction of another Railway across *Guild Street,* by facilitating the Transmission of Traffic between the Premises of Messieurs *Bass* and Company on the one Side of the

[*Local.*]　　　39 S　　　said

The Burton-upon-Trent Railways Act, 1865. Gates and 'Proper Persons' to control them were required for the road level-crossings. (*Ind Coope, Burton Brewery Co*)

traffic was worked for the first year by Midland Railway locomotives, then in November 1863 the local engineering firm of Thornewill & Warham delivered the first two Bass locomotives. They were similar to the one delivered a few months earlier to Ind Coope in that all three were 0–4–0 well tank engines. They had tall flared chimneys, with an elaborate fluted steam dome capped by Salter safety-valves set in the centre of the boiler. There was no cab as such, simply side and rear weather sheets at waist height. Outside cylinders of 14in x 20in made these useful engines for the heavy work in hand. Between 1863 and 1891, Thornewill & Warham delivered a further twelve locomotives to Bass, clearly indicative of the increasing sidings being laid down and the massive development of the breweries' output.

Initially, the first Act of Parliament prohibited the haulage of goods trains across the many street crossings by locomotives, limiting the operation and access of the Bass locomotives to the Guild Street premises and the Midland Railway Dixie transfer sidings. In February 1865 locomotives began running down the Hay to take traffic to and bring back goods from that area south of the town. Before locomotives were allowed to run over High Street and Guild Street branches (August 1865), Bass & Co used to work its traffic to and from the Old Brewery down on the Hay and the Middle Yard with its own horses.

On 9 November 1874 the extensive Shobnall Maltings sidings were worked by Midland Railway locomotives, with the extension branch opening on 1 December, 1875. Thornewill & Warham's locomotives of the 'Faery' class originated from 1873 and their later improved 'Triangle' class from 1880. Mr H. E. Couchman, the Bass chief engineer, designed an enclosed cab and No 5 was so altered in the company's own engineering workshops. This improvement obviously met with the locomotive crews' approval, so over the next few years the remaining were similarly altered by the Hunslet Engine Company of Leeds.

By 1887 the company's premises at Burton were scattered over a total of 145 acres. In addition, the firm owned depots and agencies throughout the country, with numerous maltings at Lincoln. Supplies of coal and coke arrived from Staveley, Chesterfield and several Derbyshire collieries.

Neilson Reid of Glasgow, which later became part of the North British Locomotive Company, supplied a 4-wheel saddle tank in 1899, and its last one to be supplied to Bass, Ratcliffe & Gretton was in 1917. During World War I, Nos 5 and 8 were requisitioned by the War Office and worked at Purfleet. By the end of the war, the Bass locomotive stud consisted of Nos 1, 2, 4, 9, 10 and 11 (all North British) and Nos 5 and 7, much earlier Thornewill & Warham products.

Bass began to use petrol engine tractors in the 1920s for internal shunting, to replace the trusted horses. The stock book listed 120, made up of Shires, Clydesdales and a few Suffolks. The Shires were preferred because of their heavier build and broad hoofs, but even where ridges in the cobblestones were cut, the horses often slipped when straining to move loaded wagons. Horses were also used for local deliveries, but as motor transport gradually took over these duties, the number of horses decreased. By 1930 there were only 36 horses in the engineers' department stables, handled by 13 men. During this time eight electric capstans had been installed to improve internal yard shunting.

At the outbreak of World War II, another local Burton engineering firm, E. E. Baguley, had supplied the first diesel-engine locomotive, followed by a further four from this manufacturer and one from Ruston & Hornsby. Sentinel of Shrewsbury supplied two 4-wheel chain-driven shunters. Steam was on the decline and by August 1964, after 100 glorious years of steam, there were no steam locomotives working on the Bass system. The ultimate accolade which this private railway received was on 22 February 1902, when King Edward VII visited the brewery. He was transported around the brewery in the directors' saloon, hauled by locomotive No 9. To commemorate this visit a special brew, 'King's Ale', was produced and bottled. Locomotive No 9 and the saloon were presented to the Staffordshire County Museum in 1967 on the closure of the railway, being returned to the new Bass Museum in 1977, where both are proudly displayed as static exhibits at the Horninglow Street entrance. From 1945 until the termination of railway activity, two David Brown tractors were in use as shunters, complete with 'pusher' bumpers.

Rolling stock was owned by most brewery companies until 1900, and at Burton the three major breweries of Bass, Allsopp and Worthington had their own covered vans. Some open trucks of varying types, from low 2-plank to 7-plank were in use. Bass livery was mid-grey, with 'Bass' in white script twice on each side, with a large red triangle below. The van number was in

Bass malt vans being unloaded, with one of the Neilson Reid 0–4–OST locomotives shunting a Worthington rail tanker. To the left is just visible a diesel tractor shunter with its 'pusher plate'. Sharp rail curves set in cobblestones amongst high buildings was the typical environment of large breweries. (*Bass/Brewers' Society*)

28

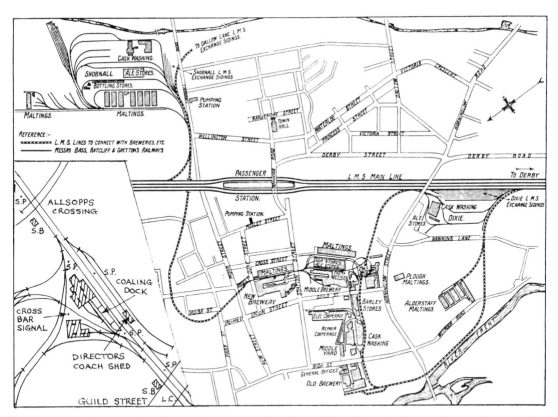

(*above*) Plan of the extensive private railway system of Bass, Ratcliff & Gretton in the mid-1920s. *Inset*: diagram of the locomotive sheds triangle at the Middle Brewery. (*Author's collection*)

(*below*) The ultimate in brewery locomotive perfection – No 3 stands proudly in its turkey-red livery, with highly-polished copper and brass on 12 April, 1948. (*R. C. Riley*)

Bass chases *Worthington* up the middle brewery triangle junction. On the right can be seen the scant protection for the directors' saloon coach, a unique feature for a brewery railway system. (*Ivo Peters*)

Morning 'steam-up' outside Bass' two locomotive sheds in 1961. The locomotive on the right is being coaled-up, while the rake of wagons weaves its way over an inspection pit between the two sheds. (*R. C. Riley*)

white on the left side, with 'Burton-on-Trent' in white at the right bottom corner. The record at Bass for handling wagons in one day was 666 in 24 hours, truly an enormous feat in 1900. During that same year, no fewer than 113,825 wagons of beer were transferred to the main line railways. The reason why after 1900 the major Burton breweries dispensed with most of their own private wagons, was the vast number required. The management and control of these wagons became so complex that the breweries agreed with the chief railway companies to discontinue with them. This immediately dispensed with the job of sorting out each company's private wagons on the Whetmore and Dixie exchange sidings. An estimate of the total number of wagons used by the brewery firms in 1900 was 400,000 wagons

dispatched from Burton containing beer, and there would have been the same or more 'empties' and inward goods wagons.

With the increase of wages and general costs after World War II, brewery use of railway rolling-stock came under close scrutiny, particularly when the four main railway companies were nationalized and became British Railways in 1948. The upkeep and maintenance of the numerous tracks, manning of the signalboxes, manpower required in deliveries and the use of railway rolling-stock all came under scrutiny, bearing in mind the under-usage of wagons due to the nature of the traffic, particularly when being returned empty. At any given time at the peak of the Burton brewing capacity, at least 1,000 wagons were to be counted on the 60 or so miles of private railway track, 40 belonging to four firms out of fourteen in 1900 and 16 miles belonging to the greatest private brewery railway, Bass, Ratcliffe & Gretton. British Railways pressed the breweries for increased charges for the use of the wagons, and this caused the firms to consider the true economics of road transport. There were less tangible factors which also now came into play, unlike the early days of Bass when M. T. Bass was a director of the Midland Railway — the new generation of directors was less motivated by tradition or for a love of steam.

The ASLEF strike of May–June 1955 clearly indicated the vulnerability of Bass's transport by rail, which was in the order of 70%. The threat of a further strike caused near panic, and Bass symbolically pulled-down the brewery entrance gate columns to allow the entry of articulated road haulage vehicles. By now British Rail was also seeing the light of day, with the vast brewery business slipping out of its hands. Discussions opened with the possibility of containerised beer handling, but British Rail would not accept the brewery companies' request for a freightliner depot. Because Bass was very much more orientated to rail transport of its beer, it was the last to change over entirely to road transport.

Trains proceeding over the Bass rail network were subject to control of signals operated from private signalboxes and ground frames. In sections where running powers were in existence they were under the control of the operating railway company. Tyler's electric and telephone communication existed between each signalbox and the head control office which was situated on the very busy section between engine shed junction and Duke Street. Head control office was also connected by the phone to every department within the brewery, also the LMS and LNER. Very strict control was necessary for the public highway level-crossings, which used the recognised bell code for the acceptance and rejection of trains. The crossings had bell warnings on the closure of the gates against pedestrians and road traffic, and many a time Burtonians were seen 'beating the gates' in their attempts not to be delayed as a train was about to pass by. A time limitation of one minute was the order, although on occasions this was exceeded when shunting was taking place. The normal load for a

train passing over crossings within the one minute was 15 wagons. The Bass book of *Rules and Regulations for the Correct Operation of the Railway*, was based on the LMS rule book. It was therefore no problem when Bass locomotives worked over 'joint' portions of the line. There were also additional instructions for particular portions of the private line.

Due to the complexity of the private railway network and the magnitude of its enterprise, it is best to refer for layout details to the map reproduced, based on the survey in the mid 1920s. There were two locomotive sheds, built of brick around 1925. Both were two-road sheds; the one laying parallel to the double-track Horninglow branch had coaling facilities, dividing the locomotive roads from the branch line. Between the two sheds a single siding, which led to the Middle Brewery maltings and hop store, had an inspection and ash pit. In the same vicinity were to be found the engineering workshops, platelayers' huts and the fire station.

The brewery traffic was classified under three headings:

Arrival – handed-over by the LMS and LNER at exchange sidings
Internal – travelling between each department
Departure – for outward despatch to the main line railway companies.

ARRIVAL TRAFFIC

Malt – the arrival traffic consisted of malt trains for direct delivery to the three breweries; due to the highly perishable nature of the malt, this type of train had right of way over all others.

Bass No 11, Neilson Reid No 5568, trundles past Mr Haywood, the traffic manager of Bass, Ratcliff & Gretton, at the 'Dehli' maltings in the New Brewery on 8 June 1962. (*Ivo Peters*)

Empties – the arrival of a made-up train consisting of empty casks was timed to coincide with an outward train of similar size of loaded full beer casks.
Grain – incoming barley for the maltings, as distinct from malt trains direct from outside maltings, required special attention, as all new grain had to be sampled before consigned to a malthouse for processing. These barley trains were worked from the Dixie Exchange sidings for storage at the Shobnall Klondyde storage sidings adjacent to the large malthouse complex.
Cooperage – the wagon loads of empty casks were sent to the cask-washing plants for normal cleansing, defective casks also being repaired.
Hop – this traffic always came in covered vans and received prompt attention due to its perishable nature.
Coal – coal was required at all locations for the steam boilers which were to be found throughout the system.
Miscellaneous – this traffic consisted of individual cargoes, normally consigned to the engineering or stores departments.

INTERNAL TRAFFIC

Breweries – this traffic was the internal transfer of home-produced malt to the breweries, as opposed to the malt purchased outside which went direct to the breweries.

There was a set timetable for this internal malt:

Shobnall	dep	9.00am	11.00am	12.45pm	2.00pm
New Brewery	arr	9.10am	11.10am	12.55pm	2.10pm
Middle Brewery	dep	9.25am	11.25am	1.10pm	2.25pm
Old Brewery	arr	9.35am	11.35am	1.20pm	2.35pm

The times allowed for setting down wagons as required and any necessary shunting.

Grain – grain wagons arriving at the Shobnall sidings were sampled by the malt department and then ordered forward to the appropriate malthouses.

Cooperage – these trains were composed of clean casks from the cask-washing plants to the breweries for filling with ale.

DEPARTURE TRAFFIC

Ale – all traffic of loaded ale trains were treated as 'express', consisting of between 40 to 50 wagons; those which left daily were known as 'Bass Specials'. Those that ran three times a week were known as the 'Scotch Specials', and went through to Leeds where locomotives were changed, with the loaded wagons going forward to Carlisle. At this point the trains were re-marshalled with wagons going on to their separate destinations for delivery the next day.

Spent Grains – the by-product of brewing is spent grains and hops, and this highly-perishable product was used by farmers as pig and cattle feed, usually sent out in sheeted-up open wagons.

Yeast – a limited amount of this product was sent out in the early days, but it is understood that this traffic ceased around 1910.

Burton Water – water was sent to other breweries out of the district in covered vans, but as with the yeast traffic, this was of limited duration. A typical day's work schedule in 1925:

Clean casks, Middle Yard cooperage to Middle Brewery, 8.00am, 10.00am, 12.00noon.

Clean casks, Shobnall cooperage to Middle Brewery, 7.40am, 9.30am, 11.15am, 2.15pm.

Clean casks, Shobnall cooperage to New Brewery, 7.40am, 8.15am, 10.15am, 11.30am, 12.30pm, 2.45pm.

Ale from New Brewery to Shobnall ale-loading station, 8.40am, 10.40am, 11.50am, 1.10pm, 3.50pm.

Ale from Old Brewery to Dixie ale-loading station, 7.30am, 10.30am, 1.00pm, 2.30pm, 5.00pm.

Malt trips from Shobnall to Middle and New Breweries, 9.00am, 11.00am, 1.00pm, 2.30pm.

Normal railway forms had to be used, in addition to the brewery system of cask-number taking and load destinations. The instructions to loaders at the ale banks were prepared by the invoicing and forwarding departments and distributed throughout the traffic department, which in turn was in close and daily contact with the LMS and LNER goods department staffs. A return was prepared and closely monitored each morning, giving full particulars of every wagon standing on brewery premises or exchange sidings, and any problems from the previous day's operation was dealt with immediately, though this rarely occurred.

To run this considerable private railway, the railway or traffic department consisted of the management staff under the chief engineer. There were sidings foremen, locomotive drivers assisted by fireman-cleaners. Head shunters were assisted by under-shunters, number-takers, signal-men, crossing-men, points-men and capstanmen. The track was looked after by the company's permanent way and engineering staff, who with their well-equipped workshops were able to undertake major refits and overhauls.

From 1865 to 1914, Bass arranged annual outings for its employees, as did Ind Coope, Mann, Crossman & Paulin, and the Burton Brewery Company. As Bass was by far the largest brewery, the extent of these 'outings' became enormous. On average there were 9,000 passengers who were transported to their destination in 14 trains. Because of the vast numbers of people going to one place, only the largest of towns with adequate facilities could handle the demand. Blackpool, Scarborough, Yarmouth and Liverpool took it in turn to entertain the guests from Bass. Mr William Walters, of the railway department of Bass was the doyen of this gathering. The vast numbers of employees were strictly regulated as to which train to catch, and it would seem that despite the free issue of beer, most of the Bass employees made it home. As the trips were always arranged on a Friday, they at least had the weekend to 'work it off'. From the town of Burton, as an example of the magnitude of the arrangements necessary, here follow some details from a programme of a trip organised by Bass in 1893, to Great Yarmouth. The number of people who took part, employees and their wives, and no doubt children, also some customers, numbered some 9,000. To transport them, 15 trains were arranged by the Midland Railway and the Great Eastern Railway, the trains travelling via Peterborough. Every employee was issued with a ticket, in addition to his or her full wages for the day. The rail ticket also included free admission to exhibitions and amusements in the seaside town.

Each of the fifteen trains was numbered, with employees from the various department allocated to each train. The first left Burton on 16 June at 3.50am, arriving at Yarmouth at 8.30am. The last train to leave Burton was 6.10am, arriving at 10.50am. After the day's pleasures No 1 train left Yarmouth at 7.30pm, arriving at Burton 12.10am. No 15 train, that for office staff, left Yarmouth at 9.50pm, returning 2.35am – quite a day!

Very precise instructions were issued that all persons must adhere to their own trains and to be punctual. Men were cautioned not to throw empty bottles out of the windows, with a reminder on the last page but one of the programme clearly stating all the licensed premises where Bass on draught or in bottle and 'Special Stout' might be obtained – all of this on top of the free daily beer allowance! Because of the start of World War I, the last trips were on 24 July 1914, when 14 trains set out for Scarborough.

6

Benskin's Watford Brewery Ltd, Watford, Herts

The date of the foundation of the brewery, known as the Cannon Brewery, cannot be traced. It is recorded as being in existence in 1750 and it may well be that it was in existence on the same spot much earlier. As London began to develop, many of the Thameside breweries which drew their water supplies from the river (which had long been considered admirable for brewing) soon found that with the contamination of the water by the effluent from industry and the growing population, they had to draw their 'liquor' supplies from artesian wells or else move elsewhere. The water of the Colne valley which has gravel beds overlying the chalk strata is eminently suitable for brewing, and there were several breweries in the Watford area, far more than necessary for the requirements of the immediate neighbourhood. In the 18th century the population of Watford was several hundred only, which was greatly increased by farmers coming into the town on market days. The breweries which slaked the thirsts of these countrymen were Cannon, Sedgwick's and Healey's Breweries.

The old-established Dyson family of brewers and maltsters then owned the Cannon Brewery, with John Dyson completing his new maltings in September 1836 on the north side of High Street, as his business was enjoying a substantial increase in trade, while there was a lull in general local commerce. In 1824 a young lad of thirteen ran away from his Lincolshire parson father — he was Joseph Benskin. He found employment in the great Metropolis and soon made good for himself, with his zest for hard work and his natural business flair. At the age of thirty he owned the City public house called the 'Crown and Falcon' and ran this as an hotel; this was to be his introduction to the licensed trade.

In 1867 Joseph Benskin sold his London interests and bought the Cannon Brewery from Dyson. Joseph was a man of great foresight and character, and with his many years of experience in the London liquor trade he was quick to realise that the London & Birmingham Railway would soon be the means of bringing increased prosperity to Watford, due to the town's close proximity to North London and the likelihood of its developing as an industrial and dormitory town. Investment took place at the Cannon Brewery, with the 1871 Census recording that Joseph Benskin at the age of 56 was a common brewer (master), employing 16 men and 12 boys. A year later a new brewhouse was constructed, increasing production from 100 to 250 barrels a week. At the same time his investment also encompassed the purchase of public houses in order to guarantee outlets for his products, these houses being chiefly in the Watford and London areas. In the course of the 90-year lifespan of the Benskin Brewery, the company empire had grown to some 700 public houses, including some in the counties of Hertfordshire and Buckinghamshire.

Joseph Benskin died in 1877 leaving the business to his widow, his third son Thomas, and his son-in-law Walter Green, who was the managing brewer. At this time the company was trading as Benskin & Co, but with the partnership of James Panton who owned the Wareham Brewery, the firm registered in 1885 as Messrs Benskin & Co. In 1894 the name was finally changed to Benskin Watford Brewery Ltd. Four years later when several local breweries were absorbed, such as the King's Langley Brewery, the Kingsbury Brewery of St Albans, Healey's King Street, Watford Brewery and the Woburn Sands Agency; with their closure came increased outlets for the Benskin brews. The Cannon Brewery underwent more structural alterations in 1897, but all this financial expenditure was such a drain on the company's resources that it went into liquidation. A new company was formed with Thomas Benskin as chairman, and so a new page in the history of the brewery was written.

In the years of growth the transport of beer became of increasing importance. Whereas the trusty heavy horse (in Benskin's case Clydesdales) had given sterling service, increasing areas of distribution called for other means of conveyance. Transport of beer by barge to London was found to be so convenient that in the latter part of the last century consideration was given to the expansion of the canal system in the Watford area. Local records indicate that in about 1870 when the rebuilding of the bridge over the River Colne in the lower High Street was under discussion, Mr Sedgwick (the owner of the rival brewery opposite Benskin's) reported to the Local Authority that:

"It was probable that relief would come from another quarter, as a scheme was being devised by which the Colne from Rickmansworth to Watford would be made into a Branch Canal for the purpose of conveying, amongst other things, beer from Watford to London, by water direct".

This scheme did not mature as Mr Sedgwick died, and following the building of the railway extension from the main line beside the Benskin Brewery, a siding was installed. Depots were set up in suitable areas with their own stables and horses. The earlier Paddington depot was closed and around 1890 a new depot was set up at Chalk Farm, alongside the goods department of the London & North Western Railway at Camden Town. Passengers alighting at the Chalk Farm station could not fail to notice the company's name painted on the walls of a large building which served as the London ale stores. This consisted of eight lofty brick arches under the main line railway track. A lengthy siding ran along at high level with an adjacent loading stage, with an office at one end for the cask-checking clerk. The company's several white-painted covered vans were unloaded, the contents were then rolled onto a Waygood self-regulating lift capable of taking down a ton at a time to the lower ground level stores beneath the railway tracks. Five of the arches, each 80ft in length were capable of storing 3,400 barrels, the remaining three were used as stables for 36 horses and hay and fodder lofts. The weeks preceding Bank Holidays saw several railway wagonloads of beer dispatched to Luton and one or more teams of horses would be sent with loaded drays. Having carried these deliveries, the team of horses and drays would return to the railway goods yard and work out from there until the railway siding was cleared. This arrangement necessitated the draymen being away from home often for several days, the clocking-on time usually around 4.00am and sometimes returning near midnight, six days a week, for

Aerial view based on an advertising sign of the 1920s. The original fine Georgian house, now a museum, stands alone, a witness to the once-fine country town brewery. (*Watford Museum*)

30 shillings (£1.50p) a week. By 1915 a similar system was operated to supply houses in Brighton and Seaford by lorry. The lorry was loaded with 15 barrels at Watford, driven to Seaford and then did its 'drop'. The lorry then cleared a railway wagon which had been sent on in advance to Brighton, before the drayman and vehicle returned home. It is interesting to conjecture the route which these beer wagons must have taken coming from the London & North Western Railway, through London and onto the metals of the London, Brighton & South Coast Railway.

The London & Birmingham Railway was opened on 20 July 1837, with Watford Junction station opening in 1858. Nearby there was a public house called "The Leviathan", named after a famous early locomotive. Watford became the junction for two branch lines, that to St Albans opening on 5 May 1858 and the one to Rickmansworth on 1 October 1862. Watford High Street station is situated beside the old brewery site, the station platforms set in a cutting, with the High Street station buildings on the road bridge over. The single-track access into the brewery curtilage curved away opposite the station signalbox which also controlled one end of the double-track triangle formed by the Croxley Green and Bushey Curves. The brewery siding ran from an exchange loop with catch points at each end, which had the houses in Neal Street backing onto the cutting. A steep rising gradient curved into the brewery, passing through a gate at the boundary in the cutting, which as the line reached higher ground then passed over a public footpath on the level. This footpath also crossed over the LNWR station platforms by a high-level footbridge. It is not certain when this railway siding was installed,

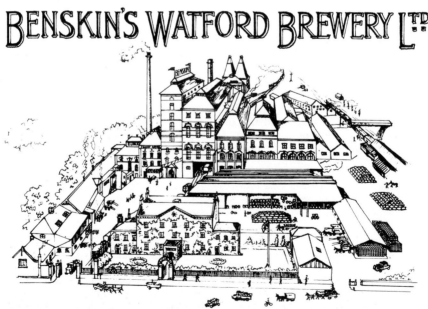

BENSKIN'S WATFORD BREWERY L.TD

BREWERS, BOTTLERS, WINE & SPIRIT MERCHANTS, MINERAL WATER MANUFACTURERS

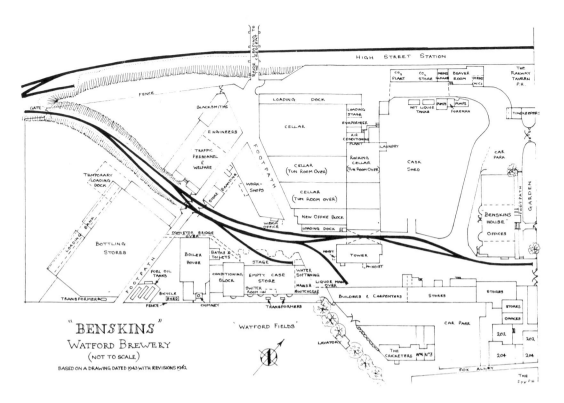

Based on a drawing dated 1943 with revisions 1962

"BENSKINS"
WATFORD BREWERY
(NOT TO SCALE)

but it is known that it was not before 1867, at the time of the purchase of Dyson's brewery by Joseph Benskin, also not later than 1897 when the main brewhouse complex was built, incorporating as it did an arch over the railway siding. At the nearby Bushey Arches, the railway bridge across the Colne valley originally laid for double track was widened in 1859 to three tracks, with a fourth being laid in 1875. All this development clearly indicated the growth of the old LNWR line, which at the grouping in 1923 became part of the London Midland & Scottish Railway.

On leaving the cutting the brewery siding levelled out, and a turnout formed a loop at the point where the public footpath crossed. A further turnout formed a short siding which served the four-storey malthouse. The two parallel sidings continued on a gentle curve crossing a roadway serving the brewery, at which point another turnout formed a short tightly-curved spur to the boiler and brewhouses. The double track came together beside the ale loading bank before a single line passed through the main brewhouse buildings built in 1897. At the exit of this overhanging building a third very short loop was formed, with an unloading bank for empty casks with round-roofed corrugated sheds to one side. This final set of points just to the rear of the main offices remains intact, it then formed a short headshunt which came up to the main road entrance gates onto the High Street. The main part of the office building was built in 1775 for the Dyson family, which before the brewery developments, once possessed beautiful gardens with ornamental fountains and a large cedar

Benskin's triple loop layout alongside the old LNWR High Street station. Note how the brewery is comfortably provided with three aptly named public houses. (*Author*)

tree. Today, this fine listed building is now occupied by the Watford Borough Council Museum, which incorporates many interesting items relating to the Benskin Brewery, also local artifacts. Across the High Street from this building once stood Sedgwick's Brewery with the 'Three Tuns' public house which was that brewery's tap house and one of 90 owned by Sedgwick & Co which was taken-over by Benskin in 1924, with the brewery being developed as Benskin's additional three maltings in 1932. All these buildings were demolished in 1965/6 to make way for a road widening scheme. The population of Watford had increased to 56,799 by 1931, one indirect result of the LNWR offering free 21-year season tickets to buyers of houses.

The grain traffic which came in by rail was carried in open trucks, the barley in sacks which had to be sheeted-up with tarpaulins. No beer was sent out by rail after 1953, although incoming barley continued until 1956, when the rail connection was removed, as work had commenced on the construction of a new bottling hall. This covered 13,000 sq ft and had a fully automatic production line with a bottling capacity of 24,000 bottles an hour. This was to be the last new building, which was situated near the old allotment gardens and the footpath; it came on stream in 1958. Perhaps the most famous of the beers brewed and

35

bottled was the strong ale, Colne Spring, brewed to the same formula as in the 19th Century and matured in casks for up to a year. This superb ale took its name from the nearby River Colne and was to be found in most West End theatres and the bars of the House of Commons.

All shunting within the brewery area was carried out by horses; one called *Port Arthur* weighing over a ton was looked after by driver G. Norris in 1904. A tractor was purchased in 1928. Subsequently two were used until rail traffic ceased, one a Fordson, the other an American-built Chase. These tractors assembled the daily train and returned the empty wagons to the exchange siding. The company relied upon colliery-owned wagons for the coal for the boilers, until these were converted to oil. Railway company open trucks were used for the sacks of barley which came chiefly from the Ware and East Anglian areas. Covered ventilated vans were used for bringing in the very large sacks (pockets) of hops from the Southern Counties. The company took great pride in its prompt delivery of orders, and this applied to railborne traffic. It has been recorded that orders placed at the Camden Town Depot by 5.00 pm could be delivered soon after 5.00am the following day!

Benskin was finally absorbed into Ind Coope & Allsopp Ltd in 1957, having on the way acquired (in addition to those previously mentioned) Locke & Smith of Berkhamsted (1913), Pryor, Reid & Co of Hatfield (1920) Weller's of Amersham (1929), Ashdown of Leighton Buzzard, and Hawkes Brewery at Bishop's Stortford. Brewing continued at the Cannon Brewery, the last in the town of Watford to do so, until 1972, when all production and bottling was transferred to the Romford Brewery in Essex. Plant and equipment was removed, the site being purchased by the Watford Borough Council in 1977. Demolition took place a year later, with the exception of the Georgian buildings which front onto the High Street, the final explosive charges bringing the last brick chimney crashing down to the great attraction of many townspeople. The site is now a muncipal car park.

Benskin's Watford Brewery was not alone in the town in having private rail sidings serving a brewery, as Wells Brewery in St Albans Road had a double siding. This siding left the main London line in the vicinity of the Watford Junction Station, and was apparently out of use when the brewery was purchased by Benskin in 1951. As with all the other breweries in the town, Wells also came into the fold of the Benskin family.

The 'Pennant' sign used as the Benskin Watford Brewery company trademark was apparently copied from a Thames sailing vessel on the instigation of Thomas Benskin's daughter, Mrs Briggs. Atop the highest point of the brewery buildings flew two 'Pennants' for some 70 years, each beside the company's name in bold gilded cut-out letters, visible for miles around. The name is still perpetuated, as the old 'Clarendon Arms Inn' has been converted since 1977 into the present day 'Benskins' company offices and the public house renamed 'The Pennant'. This is situated beside Watford Junction station and was previously a brewery owned by Samuel Roate, who sold the old railway hotel to Benskin in 1872. The last remaining vestiges of the Cannon Brewery are the Museum complex where a short section of railway track and pointwork may still be seen in situ to the rear side entrance of the car park.

(*opposite top*) Benskin's own vans beside the front entrance and 'Benskin House'. This photograph was taken between 1882 when the siding was installed, and 1897 when the main brewhouse block was built over the siding. Two of Benskin's privately owned vans in foreground. (*R. Simmons*)

(*opposite bottom*) Ale loading bank, more reminiscent of a railway station than a brewery, with a view through the tower block arch to the empty cask dock. (*Scammell Motors*)

7

Arthur Guinness & Son Ltd, Park Royal, London

In 1936 the Dublin Brewery of Arthur Guinness & Son Ltd commenced building an entirely new brewery in the northern suburbs of London, close to the newly-constructed North Circular Road at Park Royal.

Agencies had been selling the world-famous Irish stout to practically every brewery and public house in the land, with the beer being brewed in Dublin and shipped to the London Docks for Southern England, and to Liverpool for the North-West, Wales and Isle of Man. Two of the smaller fleet of Guinness ships, the *Carrowdere* and the *Clarecastle*, had been sailing to the Salthouse Docks in Liverpool since 1914. The Liverpool agency was founded in 1872. At the London end of the operation, Thomas Allen Ltd had been general carriers on behalf of Arthur Guinness since 1854, collecting the casks as London agents from the B&I Steam Packet Co, which shipped the beer from the Victoria Quay in Dublin. As the brewing capacity increased because of the enlarged markets, so too did the transport by Thomas Allen Ltd.

Until World War I Thomas Allen Ltd had carted everything by single or pair horse vehicles. Early attempts were made to speed the transport by experimenting with early petrol lorries in 1911, but these were unreliable. As with most breweries in the 1920s, steam lorries were in general use, with Thomas Allen Ltd using Sentinels. With further increases in the UK trade, the Dublin directors decided to build the new 'garden city' brewery, so Park Royal was born in 1936.

With ample space, the architects were able to design a superb brewery, complete with workers' houses and even pastures where cows grazed right up until 1980. The entire area surrounding the brewery was planted with trees and designed in the contemporary 1930s style. As a major part of the design layout, the transport requirements were uppermost in the minds of the designers. Easy access by two main entrance gates at each end of the brewery was made for vehicular traffic, and alongside the Cumberland Gate entrance a single-track railway connection was made to the Great Western Railway goods yard close by. The line curved sharply away from the goods yard spur in a shallow cutting, turning 90 degrees and then straightening in a due north direction. On passing over the Cumberland Gate level-crossing, the line split into six straight parallel sidings, each with a capacity of 45 wagons, then came together and finished in a headshunt on a low embankment. At each end of the sidings, a short run-round loop was provided. From the northern end headshunt a single siding curved along the northern boundary, then split into two sidings into the bulk filling station, also served by road tankers.

From the south-western end of the six sidings, four individual groups of sidings curved away due west to serve one each side of the malt store, for inward malt and outward spent grains. The next was a shorter spur serving the boiler house for incoming coal and outward clinker ash. The next siding split into two and served the cask loading banks and draught Guinness store. A single-road locomotive shed spur was provided in 1949 between the boiler house and loading banks sidings.

The Park Royal Brewery did not own its own wagons, hiring those required from the GWR and later BR. It did, however, have three 5-plank open wagons used internally for spent grain. These were still on the spent grain siding in 1981, somewhat the worse for wear, incapable of being moved! Motive power was provided by the GWR as required. Frequently used were 1901 Class 0–6–0PT No 1912, and one of the last remaining 1901 Class 0–6–0ST, No 1925 – both had been withdrawn by 1951. Another locomotive used was GWR No 13, a Sentinel 0–4–0T, withdrawn 1946. Standard 57xx Class 0–6–0PT appeared as well. The 12-ton vans held 117 Guinness casks, either the more usual eleven gallons or the more commonly used 9-gallon cask. The later BR COV AB 30-ton vans carry 330 casks, usually palletised, their 4-wheel overall length of 28ft 6in being able to negotiate the easy curves on the Park Royal sidings.

In 1947 the possibility of delivering the stout in tanks by rail was investigated. It was decided the road/rail tanks, which could be unloaded from railway 6-wheel trucks and then towed to customers, would be more suitable for the Guinness trade, as there were very few breweries which had their own sidings or whose bottling premises were convenient to railway sidings. Messrs Dyson supplied to the transport department seven road/rail tanks each of 40-barrel capacity. The first arrived in June 1949 and its first journey was to Messrs Thatcher's Bristol Brewery, Newport, on the 22 June. The seven tanks were used to serve Newport, Newcastle-on-Tyne, Birmingham, Cardiff, Plymouth and Devonport, and worked on 25 journeys per fortnight.

On 22 February 1949 the chairman of Arthur Guinness & Son, Lord Iveagh, performed the opening

ceremony of the use of Guinness' own two railway locomotives, by driving one of them with a rake of wagons through a tape. This was finally sealed by the chairman signing a beer docket for the consignment. To commemorate this occasion, Mr H. M. Leyland composed the following lines in honour of the two locomotives named *Walrus* and *Carpenter*.

The time has come the Brewer said,
To talk of many things,
Of hoops and staves and metal casks,
Of Hogsheads and Firkins.
And why the steam is boiling hot,
And whether tanks should singe.

The Brewer and the Engineer
Were talking on the 'phone,
A name to give the new locos,
And christen them our own.
And whether letters be embossed,
Or merely painted on!

The *Walrus* and the *Carpenter*,
The Brewer did suggest,
Together with their coat of blue,
Would dazzle all the rest.
And happy shunting would be met
By the Diesels in the nest.

The two Planet diesels were built 'just round the corner' by F. C. Hibberd & Co Ltd of Coronation

Carpenter and its crew relax from shunting duties to enjoy the autumn sunshine on the loading bank sidings. *Carpenter* and its twin *Walrus* are always maintained in excellent condition. Their royal blue livery with black-and-white lining is complemented by the large gold 'harp' motif on the cab side sheets. (*Author*)

Road, Park Royal. *Carpenter* Works No 3270, was delivered in December 1948 and *Walrus* No 3271, in February 1949. The engines are Paxman–Ricardo 6RWT diesels, of 144hp, with self-changing gearbox, Vulcan-Sinclair fluid coupling, Elcard coupling (engine to gearbox) with Westinghouse air brake system. The locomotives have 2ft 9in Baker-Bessenger driving-wheels, which are assisted by sanding gear. Top speed is 11mph with first gear up to $2\frac{1}{2}$mph, then 5mph to 7mph. The haulage capacity is 150 tons.

Since the end of World War II great changes have taken place in transport methods, necessitated by increased production, also the shortage of American oak used in the construction of the traditional wooden casks. So it was that bulk production methods became necessary. By 1952, more than half of the stout from Park Royal was being despatched in 80-barrel stainless steel tanks, being loaded in the new road/rail filling station on the northern boundary. The rail tanks are filled through a valve at the lowest point of the tank until the beer overflows from the top tank lid.

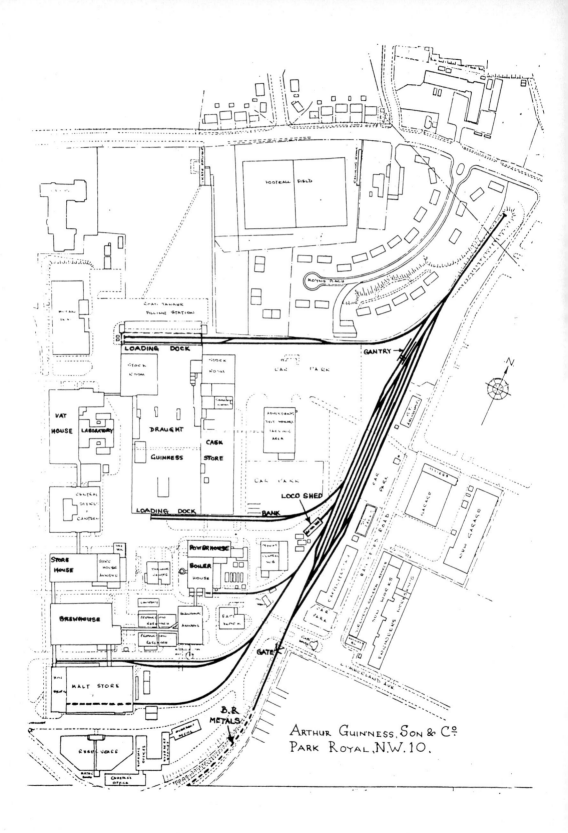

ARTHUR GUINNESS, SON & Cº
PARK ROYAL, N.W. 10.

Twice a week during the 1950s and 1960s a special train carrying Guinness stout in casks and tanks left the Park Royal Goods Yard at 7.00pm for Newcastle, arriving at 7.30am. A system in use at the time, as was common with most breweries, was to 'log' the numbers of all casks being despatched and to whom they were being consigned. When this laborious task was completed, the wagons were then coupled and marshalled in the Guinness exchange sidings to await collection by the Western Region of British Railways. In warm weather, it was essential that the casks when loaded into the wagons should be kept cool, and this was done by constantly spraying with water.

Park Royal, like its big sister at Dublin, can claim a special place among brewery railways. The private railway is the last brewery railway still to be in operation, with malt wagons being received from East Anglia and the Border Country, also cask beer being despatched to Glasgow and Plymouth. British Rail's large bulk wagons are now in full use, with 30-ton open and closed vans in regular use. During the early 1980s the old 20-ton enclosed malt vans were replaced by the 50-ton Polybulk grain wagons. Fortunately the foresight of the Guinness railway planners in providing gentle curves has allowed the use of modern long-wheelbase wagons, such as COV AB, OBA, VBA and VBB, all fitted with disc brakes.

There is no signalling on the system other than red/green traffic-light signals at the two level-crossings, which give preference to the railway. One engine 'in-steam' applies and has always been adequate for the traffic handled; the other is held in reserve and used on a rota basis.

The two Guinness Planet diesels stand on the reception siding, viewed from the Cumberland Gate entrance to the brewery adjacent to the level-crossing on the spur connection to British Railways. The first turnout behind the two drivers leads to the malt silo the second is the locomotive shed spur, with the third leading to the draught stout loading bank. In the distance can be seen the overhead gantry for loading and unloading the Irish Sea circular containers. Behind the locomotives parked on the outer siding are several container road tanks. (*Author*)

(*opposite*) British Railways' access into Park Royal Brewery is via a curved cutting from the goods yard. In 1983 the short loop to the overhead gantry was removed and the curve to the loading bank eased to take the long-wheelbase BR wagons. (*A. Guinness Son & Co*)

The track as laid was all bull-head rail on wood sleepers, but due to certain sidings being in a poor condition, several were relaid by Ward & Son in 1979 with flat-bottomed spiked rails. At the northern run-round loop an overhead electric gantry is sited for lifting of the 41-barrel capacity insulated tanks used on the Isle of Man and Channel Islands business onto rail wagons. The tanks handle not only Guinness stout, but since 1980 also Harp Lager, as a new lager brew-house was completed, due to two other major brewing concerns dropping Harp as their premier lager, and Guinness holding the largest share of this product.

It is heartening to find that the last brewery railway system to be built is also the last to survive, and long may this be so.

Cheers to another pint of Guinness!

8

Messrs Arthur Guinness, Son & Co, Dublin

In 1759 Arthur Guinness, founder of the world-renowned brewery, leased a disused brewery in James' Street, Dublin, from a Mark Rainsford. By 1825 Guinness & Co, as it was then trading (similar to many other small town brewers) decided to expand the business and looked across the Irish Sea. Agents were appointed in England, similar to those of Allsopp's and very soon trade began to expand, so that by the early 1870s, the brewery was outgrowing its original site. Opposite and adjacent to the River Liffey and Kingsbridge Station of the Great Southern & Western Railway there was vacant land available. One major problem with this site was that the considerable variance in ground level (being lower) would likely cause a problem in transporting goods between the two sites.

The Directors decided in 1874 to build a narrow gauge railway within the brewery, to facilitate internal transport. A narrow gauge of 1ft 10in was selected as there were many headroom restrictions from the old original buildings, imposing a loading gauge of 5ft 0in wide by 6ft 0in high. By 1878 an Act of Parliament was passed authorising this narrow gauge network to extend outside the brewery. In 1901 another Act authorised further railway lines and mentioned the use of all forms of traction, which the earlier Act had failed to include!

The Stephen Lewin twins *Malt* and *Hops* in the Poole, Dorset, foundry yard in 1877. They were able to negotiate 12ft radius curves with loads of 16 tons, up a gradient of 1 in 30. (*Collection of M. D. Hardy, courtesy of Mrs. L. Pitcher*)

Originally the difference in levels between the higher and older brewery and the newer lower levels was overcome by a hydraulic hoist, much used in similar locations, at the Ind Coope Romford Brewery and the St Pancras goods yard in London. As this operation was very slow, causing a bottleneck in the otherwise smooth operation of the transport between all departments, an alternative was sought.

Mr Samuel Geoghagan, the company's engineer, put his mind to the problem in 1876, and recommended to the board that the hoist be dispensed with and replaced with a spiral tunnel. This was authorised and work commenced in 1877 at a cost of £3,000, by digging a 25ft deep trench close to the James' Street boundary and forming a brick built tunnel of nearly three spirals, with a rail length of some 864ft on a ruling gradient of 1 in 40. From the lower exit of the tunnel the narrow gauge track passed over Cooke's Lane by a bridge, then on a gradient of 1 in 42, forming a zig-zag course beside the famous Victoria Quay, this incline reduced the overall height by 15ft.

Of the many unusual features in the Guinness railway, one was the method of operation. In order to reduce the number of wagons used and to keep them in maximum use, an interesting feature was the use of triangular reversing loops; there was in fact only one turntable. These triangular junctions on the lower levels enabled time to be saved, as the locomotives did not require to run-round their train of nine bogie wagons. The locomotives would pick up empty cask wagons in front from the various departments, while at the same

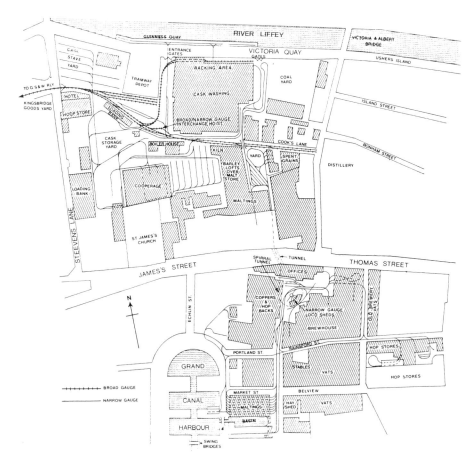

- - - - - - - BROAD GAUGE
——————— NARROW GAUGE

St James' Gate brewery boasted both narrow and broad gauge rail systems, unique in this country. Over the years the track layout underwent several modifications, particularly to the broad gauge which was extended. (M. Steele)

time they left behind the same number of empty wagons. When the load of nine wagons had been collected the train would reverse round a triangle and propel the empty casks to the cask-washing department. By using only 27 bogie wagons, a locomotive driver and his guard could move approximately 8,000 casks in a 12-hour day – no mean task!

To control passage through the single-track spiral tunnel, Mr Geoghagan invented a simple form of block-control signalling. This was before the days of electrical track circuits and lights. His simple solution was a system of levers at each end connected by a wire rope, this in turn counter-balanced by a heavy weight. To prevent entry from the other end the driver had to pull the rope attached to the lever, which reversed so as to lie parallel to the other one at the other end; the heavy weights were arranged to be too heavy for both to be pulled at once, so that the driver was unable to work the lever after the line had been blocked by a driver from the opposite end. The position of the lever also indicated to a train behind if there were one in the tunnel, simply by the position of the lever. However, this archaic 'signalling' could not last for ever, and it was replaced in 1963 by colour-light signals.

As previously mentioned, the headroom loading gauge imposed restrictions and since necessity is the mother of invention Mr Geoghagan again was called upon to solve the problem of motive power. Previously, much of the traffic had been horsedrawn, but by 1875 the first steam locomotive was in use. This was the diminutive Sharp Stewart, which was soon relegated to visitors' passenger duties, due to the fact that it required high maintenance costs. This locomotive was followed by two from Lewin & Co of Poole in Dorset, named appropriately *Hops* and *Malt*. These were rather odd looking locomotives; as many were from this manufacturer; they had no springs and only one cylinder; a feature was a prominent flywheel which was after the locomotives' withdrawal from service put to good use driving machinery from a belt attached to the flywheel, while the locomotive was fixed in a stationary position.

These two were followed by Nos 4 and 5, supplied by Sharp Stewart, which had Stephenson outside valve-gear, this motion normally being inside the frames. These were both withdrawn in 1925. The chief engineer

Guinness Dublin Brewery, with two narrow gauge locomotives used in hauling mainly malt wagons and spent grains. No 31 is a Planet diesel with enclosed cab; the other is one of the unique Geoghagan locomotives, No 15, built in 1880. Notice the type of simple coupling. (*A. Guinness & Son*)

Rolling stock for the narrow gauge network was standardised to two types; 4-wheel side-tippers, similar to those used in quarries, and the 8-wheel bogie flats. The tippers were used for the malt and spent grain traffic, also coal and the residue cinders from the boilers. The very sharp curves, some a mere 12ft radius, necessitated a 3ft 0in wheelbase. The tippers had a catch device which controlled the angle of tipping and prevented the load overturning the wagon. The tare weight was 15cwt, with a capacity of 80 cu ft. A large number of bogie flat-wagons were in use primarily on the lower levels where they were used for the movement of casks, although they were also admirably suited to carry the bulky but light 'pockets' of hops. Both types of wagons had dumb buffers, centre couplers and shackles. To carry visitors around the brewery, four 4-wheel 'toastrack' type coaches, complete with striped canvas awnings, were provided. Each coach accommodated eight passengers, who were seated on wooden seats made more comfortable by cushions, and they were in use in excess of 60 years.

had not been fully satisfied with any of these ex-stock locomotives and so he designed one himself. One of the problems with the previous locomotives was their low-loading, with cylinders and motion very close to the ground, thus picking up a lot of dirt, which led to fouling and undue wear of working parts. Mr Geoghagan's solution was to mount the cylinders and motion on top of the boiler, and so it was that his patent design in the form of No 6 was built by the Avonside Engine Co in 1882. Vertical coupling rods at the rear end connected to crankpins which in turn were connected to horizontal coupling rods between the four wheels of 1ft 10in diameter. These were powerful locomotives which could haul a gross load of 75 tons on the level, but were restricted to 18 tons in the tunnel. Other than No 6 which was withdrawn in 1936, the remaining eighteen were built locally at the Cork Street Foundry & Engineering Works of William Spence. All these survived World War II.

Part of the post-war modernisation programme included the introduction of Planet diesel locomotives in 1947. These had a 3-cylinder, 37bhp engine, with a 2-speed gearbox, giving $2\frac{1}{2}$mph and 5mph, also a reverse lever. Drive was by heavy-duty chains from a sprocket shaft onto each axle; Westinghouse air brakes were supplemented by sanding equipment. With their enclosed cabs these were popular machines with the drivers. No doubt their success encouraged the directors at Park Royal in North London to order two standard gauge diesels from the same manufacturers, Messrs. F. C. Hibberd & Co Ltd of Park Royal. With the arrival of the diesels, the previous problem of acrid smoke and steam in the tunnels was eliminated. A total of eleven diesels was in use the last, No 36, being delivered after exhibition at the Festival of Britain in 1951. As the diesels came into use, so sadly Geoghagan's Patent locomotives were gradually withdrawn, although Nos 23 and 24 lasted until 1957.

Visitors being taken on a tour of the Dublin Brewery of A. Guinness & Son in 1895. The coaches are 'toast rack' style, due to the narrow gauge railway, and like the inside cylinder saddle tank locomotive, may well have been designed and built by the engineering department, such was its capability. (*A. Guinness* & Son)

The broad gauge tramway connection along St John's Road was authorised to the GS&WR by an Act of Parliament in 1874, to serve the Guinness Brewery from Kingsbridge station. Originally worked by horses, probably limited to two wagons at a time due to the gradient once again, our indefatigable Mr Geoghagan rose to the occasion to improve locomotion at minimum cost. To avoid the expense of buying new broad gauge locomotives, the chief engineer designed another unique feature – the 'transporter truck'. This was introduced in the spring of 1888, and allowed his existing narrow gauge locomotives to be hoisted onto a 'truck', which in turn would transmit the drive from the narrow gauge wheels of 1ft 10in, to the broad gauge four wheels of 5ft 3in. This was done by rollers matching the profile of the narrow gauge wheels which were mounted on shafts, with pinions engaging on spur-wheels on the broader

gauge axles. The power of the engine was thereby doubled by the 1 to 3 ratio, although the speed was reduced by half.

The first locomotive for the broad gauge was appropriately No 1, built in 1912 by Straker & Squire Ltd of London. It was a 4-cylinder petrol-mechanical locomotive of strange appearance, with many shafts and gears to transmit the drive, which gave a considerable number of maintenance problems; it was short-lived, surviving in use for only four years. This locomotive was followed by No 2 in 1914, then No 3 in 1919, both of conventional industrial 4-wheel saddle tank design. They were built by Hudswell Clarke, with 3ft 4in wheels on a 6ft 0in wheelbase. So that they could traverse the public tramways they were provided with 'skirts' all round, in common practice with tramway regulations under the Act of Parliament; they were provided with a brass bell mounted above the frames to the right of the smokebox. A further unusual feature was that the bells were linked with the motion, giving a continuous warning. No doubt due to the regular slipping and therefore incessant clanging, they were soon removed!

As modernisation took a hold of the narrow gauge with the introduction of diesel engines, so did steam start to be ousted on the broad gauge with the introduction in 1949 of a 4-wheel diesel built by Hudswell Clarke & Co. This locomotive had a Davey Paxman 8-cylinder diesel engine and a 3-speed synchronised self-shifting gearbox, giving a maximum speed of 12mph. The wheels were 3ft 0in diameter on a 6ft 9in wheelbase; the total length was 26ft. As with the same maker's steam locomotives, the diesel was provided with skirts. Due to its slightly longer wheelbase, it tended to bind on the sharp curves, and its

St. James' Gate Brewery in its halcyon days at the turn of the century. The two horses are shunting the Irish broad gauge wagons, while the Geoghagan narrow gauge locomotive pulls bogie flat wagons, loaded with hogsheads, the largest beer barrel made (54 gallons). Appreciation of the scale and enormity of the operation can be gathered from the quantity of casks and size of the buildings. (*A. Guinness & Son*)

overall power did not match that of the two steam locomotives.

Guinness, did not own any of its own private broad gauge wagons, relying on those provided by the GS&WR, MGWR and GNR(I). For many years the various Irish railway companies provided wagons, mainly covered vans, specifically for the Guinness trade, and these were sign-written with 'Guinness' in broad letters on each side. The MGWR provided two 8-ton and twenty-three 10-ton wagons, the two former built as early as 1898 and the latter in 1916. The GNR(I) had special 20-ton bogie wagons; the earliest built around 1896 had diamond-frame bogies, whilst the later design had Fox's pressed-steel bogies. These wagons had central doors only and therefore tended to restrict the gangs of loaders, no doubt to their considerable annoyance. During the 1950s Guinness developed circular 41-barrel capacity insulated containers used in the Channel Islands, Isle of Man and Belfast trade. They were taken by road to the Sheriff Street goods depot and loaded onto the GNR(I) conflat wagons, which could take three of these tanks. Thirty conflats were modified to take these tanks which were fixed out of line due to the tight fitting. Later CIE conflats were slightly longer and thus enabled the three tanks to be fixed neatly in line.

The end of the broad gauge was prompted by the

Shunting covered vans by two CIE 0–4–0ST at the St James' Gate Brewery of Arthur Guinness. Flat-bottom and spiked lightweight rails, with disused right-hand turnout. (*A. Guinness & Son*)

Dublin Corporation requiring to make road improvements. St John's Road was getting steadily busier and many complaints from pedestrians and motorists alike about hold-ups caused by the wayside rail traffic was inevitable. Several of the 'Guinness sidings' in the Kingsbridge goods yard were lifted and replaced with tarmac to enable articulated lorries to transfer casks from the brewery direct to the railhead. On 15 May 1965 locomotive No 2 brought a train into St James' Gate Brewery, consisting of 19 wagons full of empty casks. At the end of the month No 2 was steamed again to haul out the other two locomotives; they were taken to Kingsbridge, where before the year was out No 2 had been scrapped. The diesel was scrapped a year later. No 3 was presented for preservation to the Irish Preservation Society. So the end came to this very unusual railway system, born on the need to distribute the world's most famous beer – 'Guinness Stout'.

With the severance of the tramway connection into the brewery, the transport of beer by rail continued. The large 504-gallon circular containers used in Ireland and on the Channel Islands and Isle of Man trade continued to be used, both on flat rail wagons and also on articulated road vehicles. Casks of Guinness were also transferred from road vehicles into conventional covered rail wagons, necessitating a considerable amount of double handling and short-haul road transport. Both the brewery and railway company officials studied the feasibility of alternative schemes, and eventually decided on a rationalisation of cask sizes, also containerisation.

The old Kingsbridge goods yard, by now known as the Heuston Yard, had mechanical equipment installed to handle the demountable containers for off-loading from road vehicles onto rail wagons. In 1968 this new development took place, with a 25-ton Liebherr overhead travelling crane being installed in the yard, and the delivery of some 200 Lancashire Flat Bogie rail wagons. These were constructed to accommodate two decks of Guinness kegs, amounting to 90 per wagon, whose dimensions were 21ft 5in long by 8ft 2½in wide. Their distribution within the island was to such well-known towns as Cork, Limerick, Galway, Sligo and Waterford. At these points either the breweries' own road transport or that of the nationalised railway company (CIE) carried out the distribution to customers and the collection and return of empties. Similar traffic also goes to Northern Ireland, where a new terminal at Adelaide in Belfast was opened in late 1971. Liner trains consisting of the Lancashire Flats, 504-gallon demountable tanks and Guinness' privately-owned 20ft ISO 4200-gallon container tanks, ran daily. A variation on the ISO bulk liquid container also used by Guinness is the bulk grain containers with bottom hopper outlets for transporting barley from the southern area of Eire around County Cork.

As with the newer brewery at Park Royal, the transport of Guinness stout is still being transported by the railways. In the Republic the St James' Gate Brewery is one of the CIE's valued customers, producing a revenue to the railway in excess of £1 million per annum. As part of this very happy business relationship, those road vehicles of the CIE which are used for the transport of the Guinness products are suitably signed with the Guinness logo. The enlightened approach between brewery and railway company is to be applauded by all railway enthusiasts, but it is a matter of much regret to many that no such similar volume exists in this country, other than the continuing small amount from Guinness UK production.

46

9

Ind Coope Ltd, Romford

From humble beginnings at the Star Inn and Brewery, the large brewery of Ind Coope was founded. In 1750, a Mr Cardon carried out the joint calling of landlord and brewer at the Star Inn, located beside the River Rom. His reputation improved with the quality of his ales throughout the neighbourhood, making it necessary for him to acquire a horse and dray to make deliveries. Romford was the first stopping place on the eastern side of London for coaches leaving for Anglia and the last stopping-off point for travellers bound for the Metropolis. Several Royal Personages halted awhile in the town to victual, including Princess Charlotte of Mecklenberg-Strelitz, who was on her way to be married to King George III in 1761. She was entertained at the Round House, now part of the Romford Brewery. Many years later in 1821, the body of the ill-starred Queen Caroline was carried in torchlight procession through the town on her way back to Brunswick via Harwich. The soldiers escorting the body stopped off at the White Hart for refreshments, leaving the body outside. A rebuilt White Hart stands to this day alongside the brewery as the 'tap house'.

In 1799 the Star was purchased by Mr Edward Ind and Mr J. Grosvenor, who remained partners for 17 years, when Mr Grosvenor sold his share to a Mr John Smith. Mr Smith did not stay long, as he decided to set up in his own brewery at Chiswick, with the assistance of Mr Turner the head brewer from Romford. This firm later became Fuller, Smith & Turner, the independent London brewers still in business in West London. In 1845 Mr C. E. Coope joined the firm which then became known as Ind, Coope & Co. In 1856 the company bought a second brewery at Burton-on-Trent, Staffordshire.

The coming of the railway to Romford was heralded by a Bill in Parliament receiving Royal Assent on 4 July 1836, the title of the railway company being The Eastern Counties Railway. The engineer was John Braithwaite who built the locomotive *Novelty* which participated in the Rainhill Trials in 1829. The gauge selected was 5ft 0in and work commenced immediately, although the gauge was altered to the standard 4ft 8½in

Ind Coope Romford Brewery in 1899, with the two Fox, Walker 0–4–0ST locomotives built in 1872, named *Oscar* and *Eclipse*. Note the different front spectacle sheets and open-back cabs, extra-large buffer faces to prevent 'locking' on the sharp curves. (*Author's collection*)

within five years. By May of 1839 the permanent way between Chadwell Heath and Romford had been laid, and two locomotives were in use hauling wagons conveying spoil to build the embankments on which Romford station stands. The opening ceremony took place on 18 June 1839, commencing from a temporary station at Devonshire Street Mile End at 1.00pm proceeding to Romford where refreshments were taken.

Ten years later, the Eastern Counties Railway obtained an estimate for the provision of a siding into the brewery land which is immediately adjacent to the Romford station, on the northern side. Evidently Mr Dyson of Ind, Coope felt the cost too great, no doubt due to the difficulty of overcoming the considerable difference in levels between the two sites. The problem was overcome in 1853, when the ECR spent £1,959 in erecting a wagon hoist and laying sidings within the brewery, with a further £755 being spent the following year to finish the work. Due to the increasing production and the full use of railway transport, further improvements were carried out in November 1855 'to lay down some better rails on that part of the tramway nearest the Brewery'. It is not known when the hoist was dispensed with and replaced by the present incline access, but the first recorded reference to the gradient relates to an accident which occurred on 28 September

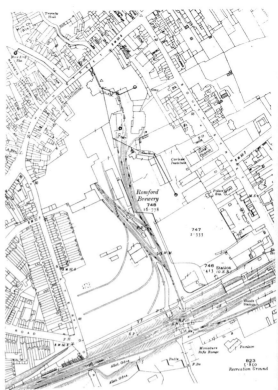

In 1914 the track layout had expanded to its maximum with numerous additional sidings and a sharply curved spur to the new boilerhouse. By 1949 a single-road locomotive shed had been built close to the footpath replacing the two 50-year-old sheds beside the River Rom. (*By permission of the Controller, Ordnance Survey*)

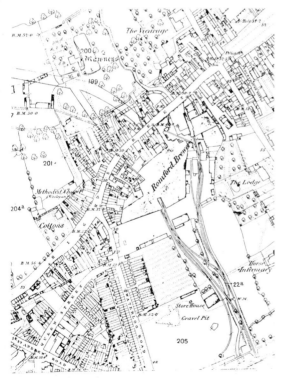

This plan of 1875 shows the interweaving track layout beside the river bordered by elm trees. Access was via a wagon turntable in the GER lower goods yard. By 1897 two single-road locomotive sheds had been provided. (*By permission of the Controller, Ordnance Survey*)

1862 'on the incline'. The first Ordnance Survey of the United Kingdom was carried out in 1871, and this shows the 'lower' goods yard with a wagon turntable from which the brewery connection ran at right-angles, passing under the embankment and passenger station atop via a tunnel. The ruling gradient is 1 in 50 with a limit of 21 wagons, the track is still intact, with the bullhead rails resting in GER chairs dated 1910 and a few LNER ones dated 1937.

The turntable still caused some delays, albeit not as lengthy as the previous hoist, and horses were in use. However, between the 2nd edition of the Ordnance Survey in 1897 and 1914, the turntable had been removed and replaced by a very sharp radius curve crossing the access line by a diamond crossing. This allowed the use of steam locomotives, and two Fox, Walker 0–4–0 saddle tanks were first photographically recorded in the company's centenary publication 1899. The head brewer, Mr C. P. Mathews named them *Oscar* and *Eclipse*.

With the ever-developing business, particularly of 'bitter beers' for the London trade, the track layout constantly changed. By 1897, the layout consisted of two single-road locomotive sheds constructed of

corrugated metal with rounded roofs; these were demolished and replaced by a larger single-road brick shed around 1939, close by the GER embankment. The 'main line' of the brewery layout ran in a northerly direction with double track and various short sidings branching off. At the north end, two sidings passed into the brewhouse, with a very sharp curve into a small yard where malt and spent grain were handled.

The River Rom divided the site, and at the southern end shortly after passing over a public footpath called 'the Batis' by a level-crossing, the line crossed over the river by two bridges and split into several more sidings, which also passed inside buildings and served loading banks. By the 1890s, two long westerly sidings were in use for cask storage areas, with the headshunt reaching as far as the footpath running along the base of the embankment of the GER. It was this spur that later became the locomotive shed and coaling siding. A local guide of 1908 quotes the brewery producing 8,000 barrels a week, with some 60 railway trucks leaving daily. This would appear to conflict with the figures quoted by Mr A. Barnard in his treatise of Messrs Ind, Coope & Co Ltd in his series of *Noted Breweries*, published in 1889. 'There are about two miles of railway track throughout the premises, and the Company owns two locomotives – the *Eclipse* and *Oscar*, so named by Mr Mathews – which bring in and take out upwards of 400 loaded trucks daily'. Total annual output at both

View of Romford Brewery around 1910, from the level-crossing in foreground across the 'Batis' footpath beside the GER railway station, to which the railway line connected. On the immediate right is one of the eight artesian well houses. Beyond the paddock can be seen the horse-drawn cart shed, then the stables. To the left, behind the white fencing is the River Rom, with the shunters shed between the sidings, and beyond, the two single locomotive sheds behind the covered rail wagons. (*Romford Brewery Co*)

Romford and Burton in 1889 was 400,000 barrels.

All the sidings branched off in a westerly direction, until the new boiler house was built around 1920 on the north-east side. This was served by a very tight radius curve which passed into the boiler house, and when a single coal wagon was delivered extreme care was required by the shunter. This building had a single tall round chimney stack, with a stone lozenge dated 1799 built into the new brickwork. During the hundred-odd years life of the brewery railway, many different locomotives carried out their shunting duties. With the inevitable progress of bulk road tankers, the demise of the railway took place. Due to considerable bomb damage which destroyed the original bottling hall, the temporary one built to carry on the business was eventually demolished and large scale redevelopment of the entire site commenced in the 1950s. On the site of the sports ground bounded by the public footpath and Waterloo Road, a very large bottling hall was

Ind Coope's Romford Brewery No 2 built in 1896, seen here beside the shunters' shed on 10 March 1948. In the background can be seen one of the gantries of the new LNER Great Eastern Section suburban electrification scheme. (*G. Alliez, courtesy B. D. Stoyel*)

A Scot in Essex; Andrew Barclay built in 1937 in the livery of Ind Coope & Allsopp Ltd photographed at Romford in 1948. (*G. Alliez, courtesy B. D. Stoyel*)

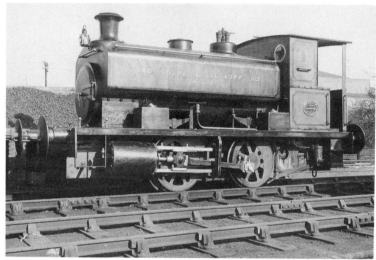

Baguley No 2 diesel in spanking new condition, shows off its Ind Coope & Allsopp company name plate and 'red hand' oval cabside plate. The arches in the background are part of the elevated British Railways station. Livery is dark green with 2 white diamonds (Double Diamond) on the radiator grill, and black-and-white edged buffer beam number, company nameplate, deep orange and gold lettering. (*Romford Brewery Co*)

completed in 1961. This dispensed with the several sidings which had served the ale loading banks cooperage and cask-washing plant. The last locomotive to be delivered new to Romford was a diesel supplied by E. E. Baguley of Burton-on-Trent in 1951. This only had a short life working in Essex as it was sent to the Burton Brewery in 1955. The remaining very light railway shunting thereafter was carried out by a Fordson Major diesel tractor, complete with front and rear metal buffer beams. This vehicle was still in use in 1982 in the Gallows Corner Depot.

Rail traffic finally ceased in 1963, although there are numerous signs of the once considerable private railway network. The connecting tunnel under Romford station is intact, as are three metal girder bridges over the River Rom in the lower BR goods yard. Two overgrown coal sidings and the incline up to the main line are intact. The brewery level-crossing-gates over the footpath are still in situ, one with the remains of the two red warning 'lozenges'. Inside the brewery yard can be seen one long section of straight rails, with several isolated sections of the railway sidings including turnouts. Some old sections of rail have also been used as protective bollards around the new North Sea Gas terminal unit.

ROMFORD BREWERY, TRANSPORT DEPARTMENT
DIARY FOR 1946

January 3	No 5 Locomotive blew safety plug, replaced by Rushbrook (fitter)
February 13 (*see Nov 12)	Order placed for new Loco shed at Willow Street Junction. Builders: Edwards & Co (No 2)
March 13	Starting digging foundations Loco shed
March 15	Loco shed site moved 4 feet (mains cable found)
April 6	Siggins & Doe (employees) carrying out repairs to railroad front yard.
April 13	Mr Rhodes of Braby's took particulars for smoke uptake.
May 15	Platelayers installing rails in new Loco shed.
May 16	Due to error by Architect inspection Pit 15, 6in less in depth than should be. Braby's asked re delivery of smoke uptake.
June 19	Wart (employee) installing electric cable supply.
August 16	Contractors completed Loco shed, instructed Rushbrooke to put No 2 engine in shed.
August 19	Smoke uptake delivered from Braby's. Rushbrooke and works dept to instal it.
August 26	No 2 locomotive installed in new Loco shed.
August 27	Works Dept commence with demolition of old locomotive shed.
September 3	Informed by 'H.B.' that locomotives are to be painted on Mr Thompson's instructions.
September 23	No 1 locomotive shed, ordered new smoke uptake from Braby's.
September 24	Rushbrooke preparing for survey of No 2 locomotive.
September 25	Advised Insurance Co boiler will be ready for inspection Tuesday 1 October on No 2 locomotive.
Ocotber 1	Mr Frost carried out annual boiler survey on No 2 locomotive.
October 14	Fitters preparing for survey on No 5 locomotive. No 2 locomotive put to work.
October 15	No 5 locomotive examined by Mr Frost (Ins) who requested application for 6 yearly hydraulic test. Rushbrooke to arrange.
October 21	No 5 locomotive. Towler's boilermakers caulking tubes and stays.
October 22	No 5 locomotive preparing for hydraulic test. Request to H.B. for new replacement for No 2 locomotive.
October 25	No 5 locomotive boiler subjected to hydraulic test in presence of Mr Frost, surveyor:- passed O.K. Railroad, instructed platelayer to instal stop at site of old dismantled loco shed.
October 28	Rushbrooke reports that a fracture has developed in the front tubeplate:- reported to H.B. (No 2 locomotive). No 5 Locomotive being prepared for service.
October 29	Instructed platelayer to cut rails and lock points at old loco shed site. No 5 locomotive put to work. No 2 locomotive withdrawn from service; instructed Rushbrooke to arrange for repairs to tubeplate.
November 9	Ordered new platelayers bogey [sic] from Wards.
November 12	No 2 loco shed. Instructed Rushbrooke to run liquor main from sports ground. (*Willow Street, near sports ground?)
November 15	Approved quotation from T. W. Ward for buffer stop near coopers shop.
November 18	Informed by H.B. of proposition for Bagguley to instal a diesel engine on chassis of No 2 locomotive, referred back to 1935 report that our gradient requires 25/30 ton engine.
November 20	No 2 locomotive. Visit from Mr Rose of Towler whom I instructed to proceed with repair of boiler for approx cost of £40.
November 27	Platelayers' new bogey delivered from Ward's.
December 16	Rolling stock. Copy of order to Browlie to fit steel bodies on our two rail trucks.
December 20	No 5 Locomotive off rails in LNER yard; gang under Rushbrooke replacing. Finished at 9.00 pm.

10
Ind Coope Ltd, Station Street, Burton

The Burton Brewery was built in 1858 on a site alongside the Midland Railway main line and opposite its coal and goods yard. Entry into the brewery was from Station Street, which gave an approach to the passenger station immediately adjacent on the eastern side. The choice of this site proved to be a most judicious one, as it gave immediate access to the railway – the lengthy rail network which other breweries required due to their scattered locations was unnecessary.

Edward Ind, who joined with Mr O. E. Coope of Romford in 1845, decided that their expanding business should have a foothold in the Burton business and so placed their roots in Staffordshire. The site selected was joined rapidly by S. Allsopp & Son immediately adjacent, thereby limiting to some degree the available ground in this area. Sidings were soon laid, with the first ale loading taking place on 13 March 1865. According to a notebook kept by the Midland Railway goods agent at Burton, the first Ind Coope locomotive began working on 17 October 1867. The first official record of the company's locomotives was of R. & W. Hawthorn Ltd Works No 2022 of 1885, Company No 1. As it is known that Thornewill & Warham supplied many brewery locomotives but that their early records are incomplete, it may well be that this earlier Ind Coope locomotive was one of those unidentified.

As with several other breweries, Ind Coope hit on hard times, so that the company went into liquidation and a new one, Ind Coope (1912) Ltd was constituted. The new management soon had business flowing, so that by the 1920s the three Burton breweries of Bindley & Co, Burton Brewery Co and T. Robinson & Co, also two Leeds breweries, Benskin of Watford, and Taylor Walker of Chelmsford and London and further south, Budden & Biggs of Strood in Kent, also the Colchester Brewery, and All Saints Brewery of Leicester, were all absorbed into the Burton and Romford empire.

Development of the private railway sidings continued with the growth of the brewery premises. A level-crossing across Station Street directly into the main brewery entrance was controlled by an ornate brick-built signalbox between two gated entrances. On the east side of Station Street are situated the warehouses of B. Grant, later Grant's of St James's, wine and spirit merchants. Because this was such a busy road, there was a requirement that the casks which had been racked (filled) on the north side brewery were loaded into wagons which were moved at night across to the south side for storage.

New sidings leading from the Shobnall branch served the malthouses, which were built on the north-western side of the passenger station, at Curzon Street. These sidings off the Midland Railway Garden Sidings were opened on 1 August 1901. The LNWR placed Ind Coope traffic on the avenue of its Shobnall maltings sidings and the wagons were pushed down to the maltings and bottling stores by Midland Railway locomotives at a fee of £100 per annum. These malthouses were converted into bottling stores in 1948 from which the world-famous Double Diamond IPA bottled beer was and still is bottled. These sidings also received rail tank wagons of 2160-gallon capacity from the Alloa (Scotland) and Wrexham (Wales) breweries of Graham's Lager and Wrexham Lager; Allsopp's Lager tank wagons also were to be seen, bringing in bulk lager for bottling. To shunt these wagons within this separate complex an English Electric 4-wheel locomotive was purchased in 1946 from the War Department; this was housed in its own shed situated in the end of one of the larger buildings beside Curzon Street.

Almost immediately opposite was the earlier single-road brick shed for two locomotives, between Moseley and Moor Streets, and clearly visible from the south-west end of the passenger station platforms. In 1900 there were five miles of private sidings within the Ind Coope brewery, with two locomotives handling all the traffic. In one year at this time the amount dealt with by rail was roughly 130,000 tons. The number of casks was in excess of 500,000; in addition there were some 200,000 cases of wines and spirits. Ind Coope was early in this field of adding wines and spirits to its portfolio, although of course this is now normal practice in the tied house system of today. The 'spirit' trade was handled by the subsidary, B. Grant, at Burton and Romford. A letter of introduction of this new facility was sent to all tenants from the Romford Head Brewer, C. P. Mathews, on 3 November 1894.

Access onto the Ind Coope private railway system was from the Shobnall Road/Moor Street level-crossing and underpass at the western end of the station. Several sidings served cattle pens and two-road end-loading dock, with the single-road locomotive shed spur curving immediately behind the gardens of private houses in Stanley Street. Four interchange sidings ran south, converging into two tracks as they passed over Mosley Street level-crossing. Five storage sidings were separated from the branch line by a large area used for the storage of casks. The branch after passing over the

52

Ind Coope's first locomotive at the Burton Brewery, believed to have been locally built around 1863 by Thornewill & Warham. It is an 0–4–0 well tank with ornamental fluted dome and Salter safety-valves, copper flared tall chimney and no weather protection for the crew. This photograph dates from 1894. (*Burton Daily Mail*)

R. W. Hawthorn Ltd Works No 2022, built in 1885; No 1 in the fleet of Ind Coope Ltd at Burton-on-Trent. (*I. R. S. Robinson Collection*)

road crossing curved into the very large storage premises known as 'Wilson's Bank', but occupied by B. Grant and used as ale storage warehouses. Two lines then passed over Station Street level-crossing, controlled by the most stylish of all the Burton signalboxes, situated at the main entrance into the brewery. Immediately on entering the brewery premises the two lines split into several more, with three separate groups of sidings serving loading banks or lucams and several entering buildings. Three sidings served the front of the largest building facing onto the main line, with one very long loading bank. This group of lines had access from the Dixie Exchange sidings area, with numerous other sidings turning out to serve the adjacent Allsopp Brewery.

On the north side of the main line, opposite the turnout to the Moseley Street branch of Ind Coope, there were two long exchange sidings running parallel most of the length of the passenger station platform. A turnout in the reverse direction to that on the southern side, curved northwards and divided into four sidings. These in turn ran parallel to Shobnall Road, then came together in a curved throat which turned in a single line around the area where previously stood the Ind Coope maltings. This single line ran round this entire complex of the new enlarged bottling hall, probably the largest single ground plan building in Burton. On the right-angle bend of Curzon Street was situated the single-road shed for the battery locomotive – this was part of a larger building. The original malthouses on this site were displaced because of the acquisition of the very large maltings complex at Mistley in Essex. The older bottling halls and malthouses were rebuilt in 1948 into the present large bottling stores, with a production of a million bottles a day, so great was the demand for

Double Diamond. Its advertising slogan of 'works wonders' certainly did for this product. The rebuilt area incorporated the latest ideas in industrial landscaping, with numerous trees being planted in several places.

The few privately-owned wagons were for internal use only, other than the rail tank wagons previously mentioned and a few bulk grain vans. Those used were painted a light grey with white lettering. Throughout the years, the policy concerning company-owned wagons varied, with a period from around 1900 to 1930 when only a few internal use wagons were in use, and again in the last few years before final closure to the rail transport of beer.

Hawthorn Leslie Co Ltd was the most popular supplier of steam locomotives, no fewer than six having been provided between 1885 and 1925. Immediately after World War II the military sold vast quantities of surplus equipment and stores, so in November 1946 the company purchased an English Electric 4-wheel battery locomotive, No 533 built in 1922. A year later, a 4-wheel vertical-boiler Sentinel was purchased, with a second in 1948. In 1955 Baguley diesel No 2 was transferred from the Romford Brewery, on being replaced by a Fordson Major tractor/shunter. This diesel was interesting as it was a rebuild of locomotive No 3, a Hawthorn Leslie of 1925, which because of its defective boiler tubes and grate was partly scrapped. The main frames and wheels were utilised and a diesel engine incorporated by E. E. Baguley of Burton-on-Trent. The final locomotive to be delivered new was also from Baguley, diesel No 3357 in 1952. Sentinel No 7 is currently preserved at Quainton Road in its original Ind Coope livery; the two diesels are also in preservation. On being sold by Ind Coope to Tarmac Roadstone Holdings Ltd, they both worked at the Wirksworth Limestone Quarries in Derbyshire. The Ind Coope livery was mid-green with a straw coach line drawn to panels, with brass relief, company name and number with red-painted background nameplates.

With rail transport giving way to the increased road services, mainly carried out by Bedford Scammel lorries, rail traffic became limited to the receipt of bulk grain vans chiefly from Ind Coope's own East Anglian maltings, also for the export of bottled and canned beers and the Channel Islands trade in demountable tanks. This limited traffic continued on a few sidings still intact within the joint brewery precincts into the 1980s.

The locomotive shed still stands, now used as a store, with just a few vestiges of rail sidings in the original brewery; those in the bottling stores complex are now covered with concrete carriageways. Where once stood the large maltings, several sidings with complex double crossovers remain, awaiting the occasional bulk grain wagon. The British Rail connection of two sidings is intact, the last Burton brewery to retain rail access in the early 1980s.

11

Marston, Thompson & Evershed, Crossman Street, Burton

The three constituent names of the company were all independent brewers in Burton. J. Marston's brewery in Horninglow Road North was built in 1806. F. Thompson & Son also had its brewery in Horninglow Road, at the Bear, commencing brewing in 1765. This brewery had a siding off the Mosley Street branch, and ale loading began on 27 May 1865. A siding to the malthouse on the Guild Street branch was opened on 19 December 1874, with running powers by the LNWR over the Midland Railway. With the increased population and rising demands in the 19th century, several brewery amalgamations were taking place and developing their trade further afield. By 1898, John Thompson and Marston amalgamated, and in 1905, their expansionist drive came to a climax with the joining of the third firm in the present day trio, Sydney Evershed Ltd.

Evershed's brewery was in Bank Square and served by a siding off the Bond End branch from 4 January 1878. Six days later the LNWR had running powers over the Midland Railway branch, and Evershed's own ale loading commenced on 17 June 1878. New premises off the Bond End Extension, between Lichfield Street and James Street, opened on 1 November 1882, on which day the LNWR also claimed its right to use the line and collect traffic.

Marston had vacated its Horninglow site by 1898, due to the limited development capabilities, and had taken a lease on the Albion Brewery in Shobnall Road. This brewery was built in 1874 for Mann, Crossman & Paulin, the London brewers, which had taken this brewery to get the benefit of the Burton water for brewing the popular Burton Ales. An extension of the Shobnall branch to the Trent & Mersey Canal on the north-west outskirts of the town to a new ale loading bank was opened for goods traffic on 2 November 1876, and this was extended into the brewery on 29

Skew girder bridge leading into the Marston brewery, over the Trent & Mersey Canal. The hump-backed footbridge is over the access to the Shobnall basin, also served by sidings off this short branch. (*Author*).

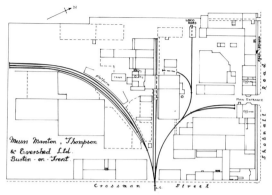

The approach to Marston Thompson & Evershed's brewery included a short spur between the Crossman Road level-crossing and the bridge over the Trent & Mersey Canal. (*Author, Courtesy Marston, Thompson & Evershed.*)

December 1876 by the completion of a cast-iron bridge over the canal, the line passing over Crossman Street. Before crossing the road there was a short refuge spur which could hold a locomotive and brake van. Then there was a turnout so that two sidings entered the brewery, whereupon two further turnouts formed a fan of sidings. To the west three lines curved and then straightened, with loading banks on either side. In the centre of the 'fan', two parallel sidings entered to the east, then diverged into a 'Y' turnout, the eastern line splitting into two. The left hand branch of the 'Y' headed due north, with a sharp left turnout serving the rear of the brewhouse, while the spur continuing ahead ran into the brick-built single-road shed which housed the two

Marston No 3 poses in pristine condition, its livery of navy blue relieved by a narrow straw-and-orange line, with a broad vermillion line to the wheels and vermillion buffer beam. This 0–4–0 saddle tank, Works No 3531, was built by R. W. Hawthorn Leslie in 1924, and saw loyal service for 43 years. (*J. Gaunt, courtesy Marston, Thompson & Evershed*).

locomotives. This was situated on the northern boundary of the brewery curtilage.

Marston's had four locomotives, all built by R. & W. Hawthorn Leslie Co Ltd of Newcastle-upon-Tyne. One locomotive in steam was sufficient for moving wagons between the brewery along the short northern extension of the Shobnall branch to the Midland Railway exchange sidings in the vicinity of Bass, Ratcliffe & Gratton's Shobnall Maltings. It was at this location that the 400-wagon 'Klondyke' sidings were situated. This extension line up to the brewery entrance gates was railway company property, and it is apparent that the Midland Railway stipulated that any of Marston's trains proceeding along this branch line to the exchange sidings had to have a brake van. A typical Midland brake van, with one open end, was sold to Marston's for £66 on 21 September 1901.

Continuing the companies' expansion, the Winchester Brewery Company was acquired in 1923. Soon Burton beer was being sent to Winchester. This was usually loaded on Sunday and arrived at Winchester, Bar End Goods Yard, on the Monday evening. The route was via the Didcot, Newbury & Southampton line, operated by the Great Western Railway. Each week there were eight to ten trucks of assorted sizes of wooden casks bound for the Hyde Street Brewery. Because of the perishable nature of the beer, first priority was given for its transfer by steam Foden lorries. Horse drays were also used, although their loads were limited due to the hills encountered en route to the brewery. The main hazard was the Bar End Road and bridge across the railway, giving a limitation of one ton per horse load. No doubt this was a much sought-after job for the carmen, knowing full well that there was a free 'noggin' at the end of the journey. The return trip took back the empty casks. This service did not last for many years, as a high percentage of casks were damaged on the railways, giving increased cooperage charges at a time when cost-cutting was the order of the day. By the mid-1930s Marston's had a fleet of 48 drays, most of these being 55hp Leylands. As early as 1929 a trial run was made with a type DG6 Sentinel steam wagon carrying 60 empty casks, the run from Burton to Southampton made at an average speed of 20mph.

In 1954 Marston's locomotive No 4, was sent to E. E. Baguley and was converted into a 150 hp diesel, and returned in February 1955 complete with the old steam locomotive's brass number and company nameplate fixed to the footplate. The final closure of the private railway came in 1967 when both locomotives were sold. No 3 was sent for preservation to the Shugborough Museum. To this day there are several reminders of this the last of the independent family brewery railways, as the canal bridge remains intact, albeit without its railway track, although within the brewery yard several sidings can be seen set into the cobblestones. The locomotive shed still stands as a reminder of happier days when it was home to the two smart navy-blue locomotives with their bright red wheels.

12

Mistley Maltings, Essex

Malt is the raw material from which beer is made. There are several areas in the British Isles devoted to the growing of high quality barley. East Anglia is particularly suited, with its deep loam soils and mild climate, and the ancient craft of malting has been carried out at Mistley since the seventeenth century.

A feature of many small towns and villages in this area is the malthouse, of which there remain many examples still to be seen. From the commercial viewpoint those maltings with easy access to the London markets thrived. These were the malthouses sited on creeks, allowing easy shipment to the Thames also for the import of grain from the Continent and America. The main malting area north of the Thames was traditionally the Hertfordshire trade centred on Ware, where it was noted in 1663 that a part of London's Ermine Street was damaged by the 'great trade in barley and malt that cometh to Ware'.

On the eastern side of the county of Essex several large maltings were built at Mistley, Colchester, Rowhedge and Heybridge. Mistley is some 60 miles from London, so in the 1850s several partnerships formed, with the most notable in 1893. This was between Messrs R. Free, R. E. Free, W. H. Rodwell and E. N. Heneage, who formed Free, Rodwell & Co Ltd.

The Eastern Counties Railway built its double-track line from Manningtree Junction to Harwich, opening on 15 August 1854. This line opened-up the small port at the estuary of the Stour into the gateway to the Continent, with the later development of the specialised passenger terminal of Parkestone Quay. To improve the communications in transporting malt to London, a tramway was constructed to connect the Mistley maltings alongside the quays. This line was built around 1870, and curved away from the upline, forming a sharp loop on a descending grade set in a cutting. This passed under the main line until it reached the shoreline, some 50ft lower from its starting point. On reaching the shore a short siding served a small shipbuilding firm, then a passing loop and a siding into a timber yard owned by Taylor & Butler, called Baltic Wharf. The tramway then meandered between large malthouses, with one long reverse siding which passed through a warehouse on the quayside. This timber building was built and owned by the Great Eastern Railway, the successors to the Eastern Counties Railway, which also

The Mistley Quay branch of the Eastern Union Harwich Railway in 1897. The descending incline was 1 in 50 on a $4\frac{1}{2}$ chain radius curve. An alternative proposal was to extend from the goods yard and to join the line beside the recessed dock. (*By permission of the Controller, Ordnance Survey*).

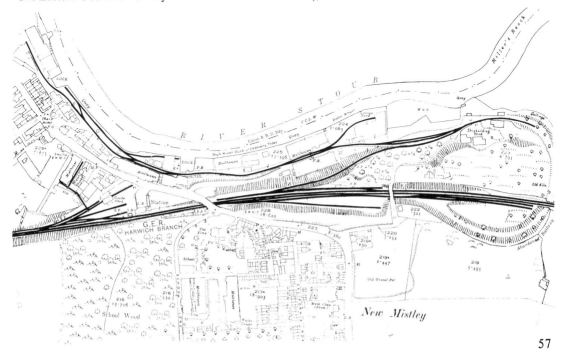

used the adjacent small dock for its own imports of grain.

By 1897 the quayside had been much improved and straightened, allowing a greater draught for the sailing barges. The earlier brickfields had closed, and the long reverse siding into the GER shed had been made into a passing loop. In the goods yard at Mistley station a turntable had been installed, with a right-angle spur siding leading off to serve the No 2 malting, with a second turntable inside the malthouse yard. This malthouse was later sold by Free, Rodwell & Co Ltd to Edme malt extracts, and is still in use today.

By 1904 No 7 malting had been built on the quayside, served by a third passing loop. Trouble with waterlogging in the cutting of the access loop line had persuaded the company to build a new access line to its dockside sidings. This left the Harwich line on a ruling gradient of 1 in 50, with a steep embankment on the coastal side, and connected with the old original line adjacent to the shipbuilding yard. A headshunt of some

Thames sailing barge *Marjorie* being hauled into the small dock in front of No 1 malting at Mistley. The timber shed behind was a grain warehouse owned by the Great Eastern Railway, served by its own short siding which passed through the building on the riverside, and on which can be seen standing a bow-ended 7-ton open railway truck. The 7-plank wagons on the left would appear to have recently discharged their cargo of coal on the dockside. (*I. Garwood*).

650yd of the old alignment on an easy incline was used. The remaining track was lifted, although by 1923 several sidings beside the main line were added. On the quayside a fourth passing loop was added. During this time a small public house called the Grapevine was serving the thirsty malsters on the quayside, but by 1928 the Ipswich brewers, Cobbold, had closed it. It stands closed to this day, its painted sign just discernible.

At this time business was flourishing, with the timber yard importing softwood from the Russian Baltic ports, and the shipyard building many famous Thames sailing barges, such as *Defender, Phoenician, Redoubtable, Reporter, Blue Mermaid* – these were all owned by M. F. Horlock & Co Ltd and used primarily in the malt and grain trade. The last Thames barge to be built was from this yard, named *Resourceful*.

Three large maltings had to be built in 1903 away from the shoreline, as all the available space had been used. These malthouses were some ten storeys high; No 1, the largest, is now a listed building. To convey the finished malt to the quayside, a local contractor, Mr Rose, was hired to move the grain in his single-horse 2-wheel wagons called 'Tumbrils', which each carried ten sacks. These were loaded on the coastal barges or road wagons. If the consignment was to be for the Midlands or northern markets, it was loaded onto the open railway wagons. These were 10-ton capacity wagons which could carry 50 quarters, or 100 sacks weighing in

total $7\frac{1}{2}$ tons, all loaded by hand.

By 1957, Free, Rodwell & Co Ltd had sold out to Ind Coope, complete with all malthouses, docks, quays and rail sidings. Today, Brooks still are major maltsters in the area, served by the dockside sidings. During the late 1970s, all the shoreline malthouses went into disuse, with new mechanised maltings being built by Allied Breweries on the landward side of Mistley station. Only the central malthouses now remain, the others at each end of the quay having been demolished to make way for modern warehouses. The line is still in regular use and is shunted by a Class 08 diesel shedded at Colchester. In steam days this was a regular turn for the ubiquitous LNER Class J15 0–6–0s, sometimes replaced by Class J19. A new company has recently been formed to handle mixed cargoes, and once more the little dockside railway has come alive again. Much of the trade handled is with small coasters plying to Europe, with exports of beer to the NATO forces in Europe via the NAAFI. Access along the quay was restricted in the vicinity of the first maltings to all railway locomotives, the shunting along the quay was in the capable hands of a horseman, who stabled his horses in the yard to the rear of the Thorn Inn in the centre of the town.

With the arrival of the railways in the mid-1800s maltings flourished at locations with immediate access to the railways. Without either rail or water links, the small inland maltings were doomed, and as with the breweries which were amalgamating, so too were the malt firms.

A former Great Eastern Railway Class J15 0–6–0 storms the incline from the Mistley Quay, while a mixed freight approaches from Harwich. The withdrawn *Brighton Belle* electric pullman coaches were stored on the wagon siding when purchased by Allied Breweries. (*Dr Ian C. Allen*)

There were several maltings with their own railway sidings within the East Anglian area including those at Bures, owned by Truman, Hanbury & Buxton; Thorpe-le-Soken by Ind Coope; Chelmsford by Ridley's, the family brewers still in business, but alas the maltings were burned down several years ago; St Margarets, privately-owned, and the large group of maltings straddling the main line at Sawbridgeworth. The latter were also served by the Stort Navigation.

Because of the seasonal nature of the maltings industry, closely allied to farming and harvest times, the agricultural workers of Norfolk, Suffolk and Essex were often out of work. With the general agricultural depression in the period 1860 to 1870, many of these workers became immigrant workers in the Burton brewery maltings, due to the expanding brewing trade at Burton. The railways made cheap rail travel possible, and by 1900, a census in Burton showed there to be at least 400 'norkies', as these immigrant malt workers were known. These men, usually over the age of 21, were recruited by brewery agents visiting the East Anglian pubs, and offered a single rail fare to Burton. This practice finally ceased in the early 1930s, when the level of employment in Burton no longer necessitated the influx of these workers.

13

Mitchell & Butler Ltd, Birmingham

In 1866 Henry Mitchell began to brew at the Old Crown Brewery in Oldbury Road, Smethwick, but after 12 years he had moved to a spacious site at Cape Hill, as a result of his expanding business. This was due to the location of The Crown in close proximity to the canal, which was handling fast packet boats drawn by four horses between Birmingham and Wolverhampton. The Cape Inn stood on the West Bromwich side and offered among normal facilities that of excellent wharfage. The other half of the eventual consortium, William Butler, also had a license in 1866, and ten years later moved to another Crown, this time in Broad Street, Birmingham. The two Crown Breweries eventually joined their fortunes in 1898, when the Broad Street Brewery was closed and the business transferred to the large site at Cape Hill. At that time the site was some 14 acres and employed 300 persons, but by 1900 the site had increased to 60 acres. Clearly this growth required improved transport, hence the railway sidings installed in 1903. The result of this development was such that by 1914 the site had grown to over 90 acres, with over 1,000 employees. To cope with this expansion of business, now one of the premier breweries in the West Midlands, a second brewery beside the original was built, opening just before the beginning of World War I.

Henry Mitchell enjoyed the distinction of being the first Freeman of the County Borough of Smethwick in June 1902. He died at the age of 77 in 1914, at the height of the industrial growth of the area and the busiest time on the Harborne branch line. At a time when many public houses were unkempt and dirty, particularly in industrial working class areas, the Mitchell & Butler firm policy was to produce quality products and to improve its licensed houses. At this time the slogan 'Good Honest Beer' was adopted, as was also the company's trade mark of a leaping deer! This was taken from an early plan which showed a stream clearly marked as the 'Deer's Leap' when the present site was just forest land inhabited by roaming herds of deer.

After approximately $1\frac{1}{2}$ miles from leaving Birmingham's renowned New Street Station on the Wolverhampton main line, a facing junction curved south. This was Monument Lane Junction of the LNWR, renamed Harborne Junction in 1879 and the starting point of the 2 miles 35 chains single-line Harborne branch. This was opened to passenger traffic on 10 August 1874 and goods on 1 October of the same year. There were originally three intermediate stations,

Icknield Port Road, Rotton Park Road, and Hagley Road. Journey time was 25 minutes to the terminus at Harborne, which had a run-round loop, turntable, goods shed, carriage and coal sidings.

The branch curved sharply left away from the busy main line on a gradient of 1 in 66, soon to cross the Birmingham—Wolverhampton canal by a girder bridge. It then passed through a cutting to Icknield Port Road station, which was closed on May 18th 1931. Continuing in a cutting at the same gradient for another $\frac{1}{2}$-mile, Rotton Park Road station with its island platform was reached. A passing loop and a spur triangular junction controlled by a ground frame on the platform were installed in 1903. This was the beginning of Mitchell's & Butler's private railway to Cape Hill Brewery.

From Rotton Park Road the line's gradient eased to 1 in 224 as far as Hagley Road station, when once again the line rose at 1 in 66 in a cutting. A short but high embankment allowed the line to cross over the Chad Valley, from which a well known toy manufacturer took its name. The final cutting on an 'S' curve then approached the terminus at Harborne. Bus competition brought about the decline of this once busy commuter line, which in its heyday in 1914, had enjoyed 27 passenger trains each way. Passenger traffic finally ceased with the 11.08pm on Saturday, 24 November 1934, pulled by ex-LNWR 0—6—2 coal tank. Two Stephenson Locomotive Society specials were run for enthusiasts, the penultimate on 3 June 1950, and the final one in November 1963. The former was pulled by 2—4—2 tank No 46757, which was greeted by M. & B's ageing Aveling & Porter *John Barleycorn*, whistling as the special appeared under Rotton Park Road bridge and opposite the brewery's private branch.

The brewery branch line was set in a cutting for its entire short length of some $\frac{1}{2}$-mile, with trees and shrubs making a delightful sylvan setting; a gate across the line marked the brewery curtilage. Shortly after passing under the A4040 main road, the line became double-track, with a left turn-out on the rising grade. The double track 'main line' curved right in a deep cutting and passed under a feeder leat to the canal. The single track line on the left reached ground level, passing a

(*opposite*) The Cape Hill Brewery layout as it was at the time of rail closure, with the later addition to the No 2 Brewery. The 'scissors' crossing was isolated for some time, with the lengthy extension terminating at the end of the sports field. (*By permission of the Controller, Ordnance Survey*).

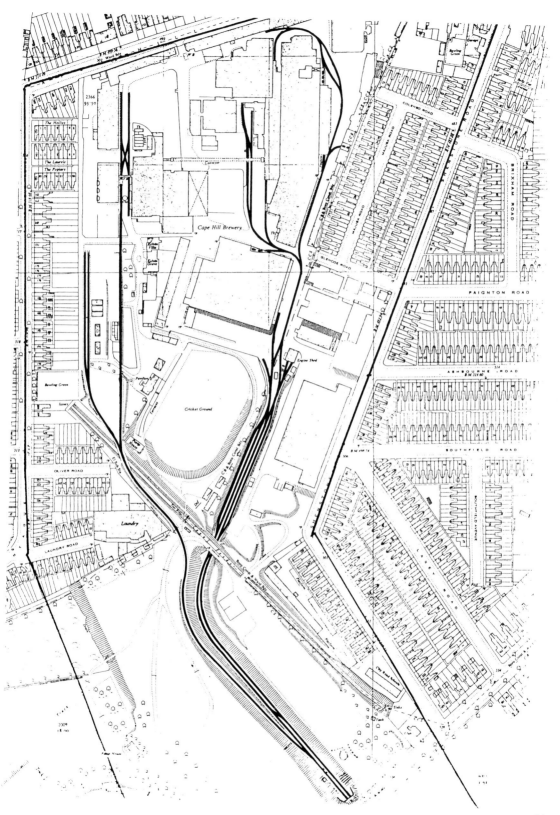

61

laundry on its left, continuing to rise on a shallow embankment to pass over the canal feeder. Immediately over the bridge a turnout turned left and as the line passed a bowling green it then formed two straight parallel sidings. The other siding ran along on a shallow embankment, past the sports pavillion and playing fields on the right, this line led into the No 2 Brewery. After passing through some trees the single line formed into two broad sidings which served the newer brewery opened in 1914 alongside the original site. In the middle of the No 2 complex there was a scissors crossing, allowing run-rounds by the shunting locomotives in either direction without disturbing wagons being loaded or unloaded. By the early 1950s this section had been disconnected.

When the double track main line passed under the canal feeder there was a crossover, then immediately the double track formed into four refuge loop sidings, running parallel in a cutting alongside the playing fields, bounded by trees. On the right were situated the stables, staff canteen, and the larger garage workshops. At this point the sidings came together into two, with one siding leading straight into a two-road locomotive shed, with shunters' huts and coal stage. To the left a short refuge spur curved round the boundary of the oval sports ground, with another siding leading off to the left to serve the large maltings and hop stores. A run-round loop then continued in a single straight siding, which then had a sharp curved turnout to the left, a further spur leading into the end of the hop store. Two more sidings formed a loop to serve the beer stores of the No 1 brewery, while passing underneath a pipe gantry connecting the two breweries. The single main siding passed alongside the loading bank, with a sharp spur turning right into the malt stores. A run-round loop split into a second run-round before joining up with the long loading bank siding underneath the lengthy pitched protective canopy. As the line approached the front of the brewery onto Cape Hill Road, the siding curved

around 90 degrees between the brewhouse and the offices, with a single short spur parallel to the road and offices, the other turning inside the brewhouse and boiler house beside the tall brick chimney, to serve the nucleus of the brewery, the source of all the steam and power.

On the cessation of passenger traffic, freight continued to be remunerative to the Harborne branch, with general goods, sand and coal going to the terminus. Brewery traffic was a major source of revenue with former Midland Railway Class 2F 0–6–0s handling most of the traffic, bringing loaded wagons of grain, hops and coal to the brewery in the morning and picking up empty wagons at mid-day. During the 1950s, an afternoon train also called at Rotton Park Road goods yard to serve the brewery, with the last train leaving from Monument Lane at 4.10pm, returning from Harborne at 7.15pm with the last of the day's general traffic. Rail traffic into the Cape Hill brewery ceased on 31 March 1962, with general freight on the Harborne branch finishing in 1963. The track was lifted and the scenic area soon became overgrown. Birmingham City Council acquired the land and converted it into a walkway, which was formally opened by Sir Richard Marsh, Chairman of the Manpower Services Commission on 6 November 1981.

The locomotive stock of the Mitchell & Butler Cape Hill Brewery commenced with an 0–4–0 saddle tank built by Manning Wardle & Co Ltd of Leeds, Works No 1117 of 1889, originally named *Frank*. It was a typical type of small locomotive supplied to contractors, this particular one was originally supplied new to just such a firm, J. D. Nowell. On joining Mitchell & Butler it was renamed *Beatrice*, and was scrapped in 1929. Four years after the opening of the private railway, the company made an unusual acquisition of a 4-wheel well tank and geared locomotive from the Rochester, Kent, firm of Aveling & Porter Ltd, better known for its road steam wagons.

Mitchell & Butler *John Barleycorn*, the strange looking Aveling & Porter traction engine type locomotive built in 1907; note the flywheel protruding from the over-large cab, also wooden dumb buffers. (*IRS*).

This locomotive had its compound 10in and 16in diameter by 14in stroke cylinders and motion mounted on top of the boiler barrel, with a large flywheel on the left hand side, partly hidden in the commodious driver's cab. It was appropriately named *John Barleycorn*. In 1925 the company purchased the first of its two Andrew Barclay 4-wheel saddle tanks from the Dalmarnock Power Station, it having been supplied new to the Glasgow Corporation St Andrew's Cross power station in 1916. This was a more powerful engine with its 14in diameter by 22in stroke cylinders and gave excellent service, carrying the name of *Boniface*. It was scrapped a month after the closure of the brewery rail system. Because of the satisfaction with *Boniface*, an order for a new locomotive was placed with Andrew Barclay, for M&B's second Scottish saddle tank, Works No 2307, delivered in 1951. It was named *John Barleycorn*, although at one time it also carried the suffix *II* in Roman numerals in an enlarged letter style. It was scrapped at the same time as *Boniface* in 1962. All three locomotives were resplendent in royal blue livery with gold names and polished brass maker's nameplates. They were somewhat unusual in that unlike most other brewery locomotives, all the M&B locomotives had wooden dumb buffers and not the more conventional large oval-face spring buffers. For a period in the early 1950s, British Railways loaned an LMR 0-4-0 saddle tank No 11221, known affectionately as a 'Pug'.

There is some doubt as to the authenticity of two photographs taken in 1925, showing *Boniface* and *John Barleycorn II* with two wagons each painted to indicate Mitchell & Butler private ownership. These photographs have been 'doctored' to exclude the central opening doors, and the company's name in a semi-

M & B *John Barleycorn*, Andrew Barclay Works No 2307, with a train load of malt, in apparently company owned covered vans, around 1925. (*Bass Museum*).

circle, with Birmingham beneath, has been inscribed in black. It is also significant that all the remaining van doors are open and are being unloaded with hop pockets and barley sacks, while the first two such liveried vans are nearest the camera. As these photographs were used to advertise the company it does throw some doubt on the validity of them, there being no other confirmation of private-owner covered vans.

As was the custom in the larger breweries during the early part of the 20th Century, the employers were most keen to bestow their beneficence to their employees once a year. The very popular Victorian seaside resorts were the mecca for the working classes, and Mitchell & Butler was just as keen as the Burton brewers to follow the fashion. In 1910 a trip to Margate proved most popular, with all the gentlemen suitably attired in their Sunday best suits, their hats being evenly divided between cloth caps and straw boaters. The few ladies who went along wore their large-brimmed floral creations. In 1924 a larger outing was made to north London to visit the Wembley Exhibition, a cartoon of the time made a pointed remark to the effect that Mitchell & Butler 'Export' beer was not available in the Exhibition! In addition to the social life of employees, the company also placed a high degree of importance to the fitness and sporting facilities available, with the large sports ground bounded by trees taking prominence, including a sports pavilion, tennis courts and bowling green. Cricket and tug-of-war were evidently popular pastimes well into the 1930s.

14

The Oakhill Brewery Co Ltd, Somerset

The small village of Oakhill, deep in the Mendips, was the unlikely location for a brewery worthy of inclusion in this book on brewery transport. However, beside the claim of this old brewery for the excellence and noteworthiness of its 'Oakhill Invalid Stout', it was unique in this country for its means of transport – the only brewery narrow gauge railway.

Oakhill lies in the folds of beautiful rolling country some $2\frac{1}{2}$ miles north of Shepton Mallet, and has many houses built of the local stone, as was the brewery and existing maltings. The brewery was founded in 1767 and ran by Messrs Jorden & Billingsley. The company went public in 1889, and a year later the present maltings operated by Courage Ltd were built alongside the brewery. In 1899 a single-cylinder Wallis & Steevens road locomotive, complete with two high open-sided, solid-wheel trailers were purchased, to transport the stout to the nearest rail-head at Binegar on the Somerset & Dorset Joint Railway main line from Bath to Bournemouth, for onward transhipment further afield. A year later a 5-ton overtype Garrett steam wagon was also purchased. At the turn of the century peak output was achieved, between 2,000 – 2,500 barrels per week. As this placed a strain on the road traction engines and with the very heavy loads which were causing considerable damage to the local highways, the district council required that the brewery make amends. So it

was that the directors decided in 1903 that the steam road wagons should be supplemented by the brewery's own private narrow gauge railway.

W. G. Bagnall Ltd of Stafford was commissioned to construct the permanent way to a gauge of 2ft 6in, and to supply the rolling stock. The line commenced at the brewery with two sidings in front of a loading bank and terminating in heavy timber baulk buffer stops in front of the offices. The track consisted of flanged steel rails, weighing 56lb/yd, laid on transverse wood sleepers secured with steel spikes bedded on local stone ballast. The line was single throughout its entire $2\frac{3}{4}$ miles to Binegar station.

The first locomotive, named *Mendip*, was supplied in June 1903, by Bagnall, Works No 1077, an 0–4–0 saddle tank typical of a design for industrial narrow gauge light railways. The saddle tank held 150 gallons of water and the coal bunker had 14 cu ft capacity. Hand and steam brakes were fitted. The second locomotive was supplied in April 1904 by Messrs Peckett & Sons of Bristol, Works No 1021. No doubt this local builder of locomotives sent its salesmen to the brewery directors with special 'local' prices for the outside frame saddle tank, having observed the earlier success of its competitors in constructing the line. *Oakhill*, as the second locomotive was named, had larger cylinders, water capacity of 340 gallons, and a

Mendip was supplied in June 1903 to the Oakhill Brewery by W. G. Bagnall Ltd, Castle Engine Works, Stafford. The four coupled wheels were 1ft 10½in with a wheelbase of 3ft 9in, and driven by the 7½in by 12in cylinders with Stepehenson's link motion. The boiler had 64 brass tubes of 1½in diameter, and a working pressure of 150 lb sq in. The saddle tank held 150 gallons, while the coal bunker had a capacity of 14 cu ft. Hand and steam brakes were fitted, also to *Oakhill*, built by the local Bristol firm of Peckett. (*Robin Atthill*)

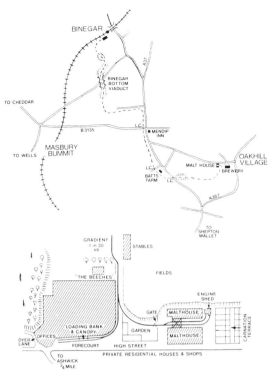

DIAGRAM OF THE RAILWAY SERVING
THE OAKHILL BREWERY; c 1920.

Route layout and plan of the only brewery narrow gauge system in England, set in the lovely Mendip hills of Somerset. The Binegar terminus by the S&DJR had a two-road interchange facility in a shed with the standard gauge siding. (*M. Steele, Author*).

(*below*) Oakhill Brewery at the turn of the century, with a full trainload of cask and beer cases loaded up at the bank, awaiting the signal to proceed to Binegar. (*A. Barnett*).

coal bunker to take 5 cwt. As with *Mendip*, both steam and hand brakes were fitted. *Oakhill*'s 2ft 3in driving wheels with a wheelbase of 4ft 3in compared with *Mendip*'s 1ft 10½in driving wheels on a 3ft 4in wheelbase.

Six low-sided bogie wagons were supplied by Bagnall as part of its overall deal. They were 20ft 0in long by 5ft 6in wide, running on two 4-wheel channel-form bogies with cast-iron centre privots, a 2ft 6in wheelbase with 1ft 3in diameter cast-iron wheels. Bogies were at 14ft 0in centres. The underframe was of steel channels 6in x 3in x $\frac{3}{8}$in, well trussed, with centre couplings in typical narrow gauge style. A platform at one end was provided for a brakesman, who could apply the handbrake to the four wheels on the bogie beneath him. The wagon sides were built of three pine planks, with a central 4ft 0in wide door. Carrying capacity was eight tons, the tare of the bogie wagons was four tons. They carried a light grey livery to the bodywork, with all metalwork painted black. Trains were normally made up of four wagons, although in peak times the more powerful *Oakhill* could take five wagons, each carrying twenty-four 36-gallon barrels, making a gross load of 50 tons. The average speed was 10mph, with two to four trips per day, but at peak times as many as six were made. Running time on the up grade to Binegar was 25 minutes, the return to Oakhill with the empties taking around 20 minutes.

The following is a description of a journey from the Oakhill Brewery to the S&DJR Binegar station, with present day observations as to the remains of the trackworks to be seen.

Loading up to the four bogie bolster wagons took little more than an hour at the loading bank under the overhanging canopy. Harry Lambert, the driver, who still lives in the village as does Arthur Barnett whose turn it may have been, checked the load of barrels,

kilderkins, firkins and pins of Double Stout Invalid Porter and Brown Stout Porter, to ensure that they were safely loaded. The barrel sizes were loaded in three rows of eight, with the smaller sizes assorted in their loading, sometimes being sheeted-up with a tarpaulin. When all was correct, the driver entered his cab with his fireman, whilst the brakemen climbed onto the platform of the rear bogie wagon. While loading-up had been carried out, the locomotive had built up a good head of steam, after the fire had been lit early that morning. The engine had run down light from the engine shed up by the malthouses and backing onto the cottages of Carnation Street. The locomotive had then backed down the short side street onto its train. Steam pressure was now such that the safety-valves were blowing-off, and with a 'pip' on the whistle and a hiss of escaping steam as the drain-cocks were blown-off, the train slowly moved foward around the angled corner of the brewery. This curve was of 30 chains radius and was the sharpest on the system, the remainder being of 80ft radius. Creaking and groaning round the left curve the train proceeded up the side street, hugging the rough hewn local stone building of the brewery. A short way up this building there was situated a water supply for the use of the locomotives. As the brewery buildings were left behind us, caution was still required as we negotiated the set of points which led to the malthouses and engine sheds. This point was opposite the brewery owner's house named *The Beeches*. The siding leading away to our right passed through a walled garden, with a gate at each end over the railway track. On passing out of the garden this siding rose gradually across an open courtyard in front of the two malthouses which still exist in use to this day. As the line crossed the yard a further point formed two parallel sidings which then passed between the two buildings, passing under covered awnings, pipework and angled 'bridge'. At the far end the two sidings curved sharply left and thence entered two adjacent engine sheds, the left-hand one set back a few feet shorter than the other. The high doors and lintels indicated their original purpose in housing the two steam road wagons. Between the rails are recessed inspection pits, having served in their time steam wagons, steam railway locomotives and now petrol and diesel vehicles. These two locally stone-built sheds with red brick quoins stand intact, still being used for transport maintenance purposes. The two malthouses remain almost as they were some 60 years ago, but with the addition of a modern silo to the rear.

As the heavily loaded train passed the owner's house, the steep gradient of 1 in 30 began. The engine exhaust now barked, resounding between the trees and the stable blocks now divided up into several residential properties. The line continues more or less in a due westerly direction in a straight line, with a hedgerow on the right and a 5-strand wire fence to the fields on the left. The line then turns right, where derailments often occurred, but not on today's journey, although we have two jacks on our footplate, just in case. As the line passes between a hedgerow forming two fields, we rumbled over a 6ft span steel girder bridge over a small stream, the two parallel girders and a few sleeper spikes are still intact. The line now continues on its steady climb as the engine pounds away, chasing away the grazing cows from beside the track. The firm ballasted trackway is still in excellent condition, as is the 3ft high gently curved embankment which leads up to the first level crossing. The line crosses over the A37 Shepton Mallet — Bristol main road on a diagonal, with the remains of an old wooden gate still to be seen beside the newer tubular metal farm gates.

With the approach of the train to the level-crossing we reduce speed to a walking pace in order that the fireman can jump down off the footplate and to run forward to open the two gates. A blast on the whistle warned the spasmodic road traffic that our train was about to cross over on seeing the way clear with a wave from our fireman. As the train passes over, it's then the turn of the brakesman to close the two gates to the fields behind him, leaving the road clear once again.

The line now takes a north-westerly direction passing through Batts Farm, shortly passing over a farm track and then coming alongside the hedgerow of the A37 main road. The gradient had now eased somewhat, although still on an upward climb to the summit as we approached the Mendip Inn, having climbed 100ft in the first mile. This public house situated at a crossroads was formerly an Oakhill Brewery house, now a part of the Courage Group. Opposite in a small copse may still be seen the pointed wood railway boundary fence posts at the point where the second main level crossing was situated. Again a long blast on the whistle and the same procedure as before was enacted as the line crossed what is now the B3135 secondary road. The railway track now hugged alongside the hedgerow of the main road for several more fields, until it reached a lane. Turning 90 degrees left and once again in a westerly direction, the narrow rails keep to the left-hand side of the lane on a more or less level gradient. High trees and shrubs now form an overgrown avenue, but signs of the old sleeper indentations may still be discerned. On leaving the lane the track turned north across a field, with an embankment increasing until the railway bursts out into the head of a lovely small valley.

We now slowly crossed over the railway's major construction, a three span steel girder viaduct which crossed Binegar Bottom, 35ft below rail level. The 40ft spans were supported on rough faced random-sized stone piers, quarried from a quarry within a stone's throw distance. The remains of one of these piers may still be seen alongside the small road which winds its way up this delightful valley on its way to the cathedral city of Wells. On reaching the far side of the valley, the line curved to the right on a gently curving embankment with trees on the north side of the valley. Midway on this now very overgrown embankment of some 20ft height was an underbridge giving access to fields. The same rough-hewn stone used in the bridge abutments are still in situ, although the steel girder bridge has long since been removed. As the line reached the level of the

fields which also form the parish boundary, the line then curved slightly to the left in a north-westerly direction as it entered the railway's only cutting. This is only a short cutting of no more than six foot in depth, now overgrown, but still bounded by the railways wood posts. As the train entered the cutting, the driver gave a blow on the whistle to warn of the trains approach to Binegar Station.

Oakhill and Somerset & Dorset Joint Railway staffs have been warned of our approach as we chugged along nearing the main line railway. This could be seen coming in from our left as we gently curved to the right as our line came in alongside that of the standard gauge. The throat of the goods yard to the main line was now on our left as our narrow gauge track finally straightened out in a north-easterly direction. Crossing slowly over a point we take the left-hand siding which runs parallel to the 'spare' siding, both running into the terminus shed. This consisted of a half round-headed shed built of corrugated metal sheets to the roof, supported on metal 'V' purlins and joists resting on the right-hand side a solid stone wall to the full height. The left-hand side has eleven stone piers, with a timber platform loading bank running three-quarters of the length from the dead end. Situated at this far end was a timber boarded shed which acted as the Goods Agent's office and staff messroom. At a later date a timber 2-ton derrick crane was installed on the loading bank with a heavy supporting timber roof beam. The end of this shed backs onto the station master's garden.

The standard gauge siding ran alongside the loading dock on the outside, and as soon as the Oakhill train had pulled in and brakes had been applied, so several

Oakhill trundles across the viaduct at Binegar Bottom with its short train load. The low-sided wagons were 20ft long by 5ft 6in wide, running on two 4-wheel cast-iron bogies. with 15in diameter wheels on a 2ft 6in wheelbase, placed at 14ft centres. Centre couplings were provided, as also was a small platform for the brakesman at one end; the brake acted on all four wheels of one bogie. A 4ft central door allowed twenty-four 36-gallon barrels to be loaded, a gross load of 8 tons, Trains were usually made up of four wagons, with between two and four trains per day, taking 25 minutes on the up grade to Binegar, returning empties in 20 minutes. (*IRS*).

men immediately set upon the narrow gauge wagons. Centre doors were dropped down onto the loading bank and the casks rolled out across the timber platform and into the two or three standard gauge 10- or 12-ton trucks. Now was the time for the driver to relax, but for the fireman there was plenty of work still to do. First, a top-up of the water into the saddle tank, then a rake out of the fire grate to remove ash and clinker, then the now bright fire was topped-up with best coal, probably from the local Somerset coalfields at nearby Radstock. The steam pressure gauge was now fairly low after the hard climb, and the time now spent in unloading the beer casks would be well spent in building pressure up once again. As soon as this unloading had been completed, probably on this the first train of the day by 10.00am, the return journey of some twenty minutes would commence. During the school holidays it was not uncommon for children to take an unofficial ride back down to Oakhill village, and what great fun that must have been!

_____

Binegar station and goods yard in the early 1960s on the former S&DJR Bath to Bournemouth line. The long shed on the right was the terminus and interchange point of the Oakhill Brewery narrow gauge railway, which ran for some 2¾ miles in an easterly direction. This corrugated roofed building was still in use by the local coal merchant, as seen in this view. (*K. F. Marchant, courtesy Robin Atthill*).

The transfer shed remains intact, witness to its age having had some of the end roof sheets removed to enable the local coal merchant to load up a sack-filling machine with the use of a diesel tractor. The typical S&DJR station master's house is intact, with the last incumbent of this position now enjoying his retirement in residence. The approach road leading up to the station yard and platform beside the abutments of the railway overbridge at Binegar is still used. In the old goods yard several loading docks are to be seen in among the vegetation which is now taking over, much to the delight of naturalists who will observe such butterflies as Peacocks, Red Admirals, Fritillaries, Tortoiseshells and Common Blues. The Oakhill Brewery Railway is still determined not to be forgotten even after some 55 years has elapsed since those two fine locomotives, *Mendip* and *Oakhill*, had finally played

their part in this country's transport history. The 'Breezy Mendips' are the poorer for their loss. Since the last standard gauge train on the Somerset & Dorset Joint Railway on Sunday 6 March 1966 had passed through Binegar Station the trackbed is reverting back to nature, just as the brewery railway has done.

As the railway officially did not carry any passengers, nor required any compulsory powers to purchase land for its construction — this belonging to the brewery directors — no Parliamentary authority was required. Trade started to decline at the end of World War I, and with the rise of the internal-combustion engine drays, the line was closed in 1921. Soon after the line was lifted and with the rolling stock was sold to the contractors, who were at that time building the famous Barry Docks in South Wales. It is recorded that the locomotive *Oakhill* survived to at least 1949, when it was observed working at the Penarth Cement Works in Glamorgan, also in the Principality of Wales. In 1925 a fire severely damaged the brewery which had to close down — however, a small section of the original buildings either side of Dye Lane are extant. The malthouses further up High Street are still operated by the Courage Group, which purchased them from Bristol United Breweries.

15

Snape Maltings, Suffolk

Meandering through the rolling hills of mid-Suffolk the River Alde, with its source at Brandish, opens out into a typical East Coast broad estuary. At Snape Bridge, five miles as the crow flies from the North Sea, the river is tidal. The tortuous course of the Alde on its way to the Sea, takes a further 20 miles to reach the sea at Orford Haven, having passed the old ports of Iken, Aldeburgh and Orford, and the lengthy shingle bar holding back the River Alde where it changes name to the River Ore. The broad estuary is the home of many water birds who revel in the lush Norfolk reed beds and mudflats.

Of the many small ports once along this coastline, Snape Quay is remarkable in that it survives to this day little changed from Victorian times. The visitor today may still see the spritsail and topmast, with its distinctive deep red sails of the Thames sailing barge moored at the Quay, much as 100 years ago. This harbour has not been spoilt by modern development, although the large malting business which flourished here for 150 years is but a shadow of its former past. The Snape Maltings today are better known as the home of the music festivals and concerts, held in the largest of the old malthouses facing seaward, and made famous by Benjamin Britten.

Around 1800 there was a small business centred around the Quay, receiving and distributing coal to the local community, and shipping out corn and hay to the London markets. At the nearby town of Leiston, Richard Garrett & Sons carried on the business of agricultural engineers, producing farm implements and steam road wagons. Grandsons of the founder grew up in the age of the industrial revolution, with the third

Richard carrying on the Leiston Works Engineering, with brothers Balls Garrett owning the Medway Iron Works at Maidstone, and Newson Garrett purchasing the Snape business. At the death of their father in 1837 the inheritances were divided, with Newson at the young age of 29 in 1841 purchasing the Snape business of Osborne & Fennell, corn and coal merchants of Snape Bridge.

By 1844 Newson Garrett had expanded the shipping business with a recorded annual 17,000 quarters of barley sent out on the sailing barges for delivery to the London breweries. It was not long before Newson decided that not only could he profitably send out barley for malting at other locations, but that he could carry out that lucrative business as well. So it was that he designed and had built further buildings in 1854, suitable for malting on this site. The bricks were from local brickfields in which he also had a financial interest, the mellow red facings set off by yellow brick quoins. There is a wall plaque with this date clearly to be seen, also earlier cast iron wall tie plates with the inscription 'Newson Garrett Freehold 1846'; these were cast by his brother Richard at the Leiston foundry. The site rapidly expanded, not only with malthouses, but also increased port facilities, carpenters' shop and smithy. Dock and repair facilities were constructed, with the first known 'Thames' type sailing barge called *Agro*, being built at

Drawing by Beverley Peaty of the attractive façade of the Snape Maltings, with an empty coal wagon leaving the archway and turntable for the level-crossing into the station yard. (*Beverley Peaty*).

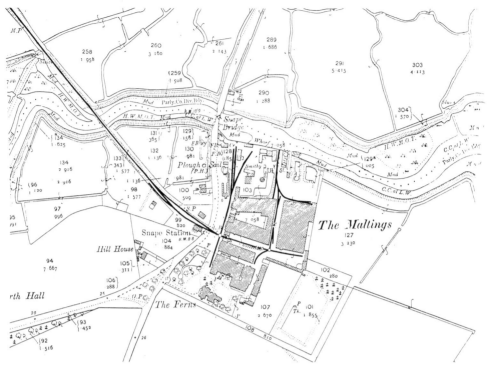

Snape Maltings set in its delightful estuary setting. The short headshunt up to the wharf also served the dock, where Thames sailing barges were once built. (By permission of the Controller, Ordnance Survey).

Snape in 1858. This was of 51 tons and worked for Newson Garrett until 1897, when it was broken-up.

Newson Garrett was an energetic and dynamic Victorian gentleman, and on his instigation and insistence coupled with the guarantee that he would give regular freight to a railway connection to his malting

Great Eastern Railway's Holden Class Y14, hauling a freight only train known locally as the 'Snape Express', over the River Alde timber trestle bridge, which had a speed limit of 15mph. (Suffolk Record Office).

business, The East Suffolk Railway Company obtained an Act of Parliament in 1854 to construct a single-track branch line to Snape Bridge. Newson had realised fully the potential of the railways, and that this means of transport for his products was going to broaden his markets and displace the slow but reliable sailing barges.

Snape Junction was built on the double-track main line from Ipswich to Yarmouth, three miles south of Saxmundham and north of the Framlingham branch line, with early intentions of building a passenger station, which now seems remarkable due to the isolated position and sparse farming community in the locality. The line veered away in an easterly direction on

a falling gradient of 1 in 53, with a siding on the up and down side, controlled by a small signalbox and a fixed distant on the branch approach to the main line. The branch followed the northern side of the River Alde valley in a near straight line, with a shallow curve near the centre of its 1 mile 32 chains, crossing several drainage dykes before reaching the 3-span timber trestle bridge over the Alde, just prior to fanning out into the Snape goods station. The line was opened for a daily goods traffic on 1 June 1859, and carried inward traffic of grain, coal and coke, lime and general merchandise for the farming community. The outward traffic was primarily malt in sacks, also sugar beet for the factory at Ipswich. On 7 August 1862 the Great Eastern Railway Company took over from the ESR. A route availability of 1 was in force, limiting the speed to 15mph, due to the lightweight construction of the timber culverts and river bridge.

The branch line was built for goods traffic only and had no provision for passengers. The only known occasion when a passenger train did visit this line was the 'Suffolk Venturer' visit in 1956, when five bogie coaches were hauled by a Class E4 2–4–0 (Route Availability 2) for a rail enthusiasts' special. Snape station house is a typical East Anglian yellow-brick structure built for the station master and goods agent, who for many years was one William Everritt. This building is still intact and has recently been renovated and is in use as a private residence. Across the trackbed stands a more recent small brick building, now vandalised, but still clearly showing its railway ancestry which was used as a shunters' and goods office. This was located alongside the unprotected level crossing across the B1069 road and malting forecourt approach. In the railway-owned goods yard the sidings were minimal, with one short siding and one run-round facility, albeit not for the locomotives, as they worked engine first towards the main line and their Ipswich depot. On crossing the public highway, the two lines converged onto a wagon turntable immediately in front of the impressive arched entrance into the inner courtyard of the Maltings. The turntable had a siding running at right-angles to the entrance siding, running in each direction, fronting onto the long line of the attractive façades of the malthouses and offices. Here there are situated several lucams used for hauling up the sacks of barley to the tops of the buildings, and likewise loading up the railway vans with malted grain. At the end of this line of buildings, the single siding split into a further two which reached to the quayside, enabling the sailing barges to load direct into railway vans, assisted by a small hand-operated crane, whilst conveniently passing the back door of the Plough and Sail public house. The main siding which passed through the curved arch entrance with its 1859 dated and initialled keystone, served a long loading bank with metal corrugated canopy over for the coal traffic, situated in the broad inner courtyard. A second wagon turntable in the centre of the malthouse complex had three rail spurs off it. The primary siding of these three ran parallel to

Snape Maltings archway with wagon turntable in the foreground, and the long siding running across parallel to the front façade. Through the arch can be seen the coal dock. Note the stub end points. (*Suffolk Record Office*).

the siding at the front of the main buildings, passing between two long lines of malthouses, the one on the seaward side now in use as the music concert hall. This siding then formed two further sidings before terminating at the quayside as described. This second siding came alongside the repair and boatbuilding dock and engineers workshop, now in use as the Snape Craft Shop; this siding had two reverse sidings, one curving sharply to serve the largest and most recently built malthouse.

The motive power for the line throughout its life were the ubiquitous Class J15 0–6–0 tender locomotives with their earlier stovepipe chimneys; these were shedded at Ipswich. During the World War II several unusual formations were seen, with war damage debris being taken along the line with a J15 at each end of the trains, two engines being required because of the steep gradient approach to Snape Junction. On at least one occasion a Paxman diesel did venture onto the line, but had the ignomy of failing just as it reached the trestle bridge over the Alde, and it was with much delight to the locals when an old six-coupled tender engine had to be called to its assistance. The Snape branch was often rostered in with both the two nearby branch lines to Framlingham and particularly to Leiston and Aldeburgh, and bonus systems ensured no 'hanging around' by locomotive crews.

Delightful rural scene in 1959 of Class J15 0–6–0 No 65478 leaving Snape Station, with the fine maltings façade in the background. (*Dr Ian C. Allen*).

Snape Junction scene taken in 1962 from the signalbox, with a Class J15 0–6–0 awaiting the right of way onto the Ipswich/Saxmundham main line. (*Dr Ian C. Allen*).

The usual goods train approaching Snape Junction from the Ipswich direction intending to proceed to Snape Maltings would have been controlled by the signals opposite the signalbox. These would have indicated whether the train was to draw forward over the farm lane level-crossing, and to reverse back into the lay-by siding off the up line, if it was required to give a free line ahead to any train close behind it. If the way was clear in both directions, the goods train reversed back over the crossover onto the down line and past the signalbox. The points would then be set for the Snape branch line and the train could then proceed forward. Trains coming from the Saxmundham direction also passed the signalbox and then had the same option, either to reverse back into the refuge siding off the down line, or to reverse straight back down the branch line. For several years just after the last war, when a Class

J15 0–6–0 from Ipswich was not available, a Class J17 was used, in which case it left any trucks for the Snape branch at one of the two parallel sidings. The Framlingham branch locomotive would then be sent to take the trucks to the terminus, this task usually rostered to the Class F3 2–4–2 tank engines. Their route availability was 3 and therefore special permission had to be granted, with extra attention to the speed limit.

Locomotives were not authorised to cross the highway, although this did happen on occasions when more than an average number of trucks was to be shunted. The duty of transferring wagons into the malting complex was carried out by a horse-shunter for most of the life of the railway, only finally giving way to a diesel tractor in the last few remaining years. Within the malting company premises, at least one ex-GER van was used for internal purposes only, reputed at one time to be of the dumb-buffer type. The barley and malt traffic lasted until 1950, giving way to diesel lorries, just as the sailing barge traffic eventually had to give way to the steam railways. The line remained open for the once-a-day goods train bringing in coal and coke for another 10 years, finally closing on 7 March 1960.

Signalling on the branch line originally had two

signals for each direction. On the approach to Snape Goods Yard, a distant gave warning of the imminent approach before the River Alde bridge. There was also one situated close to the stationmaster's house, controlling the road-crossing. In the reverse direction, a distant gave warning of the approach to the junction; this first signal was situated at the beginning of the rising gradient. Around the curve near the signalbox was the second signal. In latter years the three former signals were dispensed with, and only the fixed distant in the latter position gave a reminding warning to the driver of the junction; as if he needed it, having had to open-up to breast the steep gradient!

Back to the earlier days of the Garrett family, when Newson died in 1893 at the ripe old age of 81 he divided his malting business equally between his children. His youngest son, George, continued to manage the maltings until 1964, whilst Edmund became the manager of the Bow Brewery in London. He later became a partner in the brewing business with Mr Smith, it being renamed Smith's Garretts. This East End Brewery was later bought-out by Taylor Walker, the other East London brewery situated at Limehouse. It in turn became a part of Ind Coope in 1959, although the Bow Brewery had long disappeared, giving way to the public house named the Bombay Grab, beside the modern Bow Flyover approach to the church of Bow Bells fame. In the earlier days of Newson Garrett's malting development, three to four barges were often to be seen tied up at his wharf, and with his enthusiasm for building and engineering, Newson purchased a steam driven-barge called *Katherine*. Evidently this was a successful venture, and he purchased a sister steam barge, the *Gladys*. Barges continued to visit the Snape Maltings wharf until the outbreak of hostilities in 1939. After a lapse of some 26 years, the 100-ton barge *Atrato* brought back some commercial life to the quay with a cargo of barley to be malted from Lowestoft in 1965. This limited commercial traffic continued only for five more years, the *Redoubtable* being one of the most commonly seen sailing barges.

In 1918 Newson's youngest son, George, who had been malting manager since 1882, finally merged with the malting company of Messrs S. Swonnell & Sons, of Oulton Broad, Lowestoft, Suffolk. He had been steadily purchasing shares of this competitor, also shares of railway companies such as the Central Argentine Railway Company and the United Railway of Havana, Cuba. Swonnell's Oulton Broad maltings, in two large blocks alongside the Broads, were served by wharves for the sailing barges, also a siding curved away from a long siding leading from Oulton Broad station, which also had a spur leading into another malting across the water from Swonnell's. On entering Messrs S. Swonnell's curtilage, the single siding divided into two, one each serving the malthouses; one with a run-round loop, the other with a reverse headshunt. At this site, several years after closure of the rail sidings, one of Swonnell's 6-plank 10-ton open wagons was found. This had open-spoke wheels with brakes and levers on one side only, and had been painted red oxide to bodywork and solebar, with white lettering, shaded black, reading 'S. Swonnell & Sons Ltd' with '20' and 'Snape' in white only; tare weight was 5tons 14qr 1lb, load 10 tons.

In 1952 a small extension was built on the front façade behind the public house, alongside a section built in 1885, as indicated in both cases by carved dated stone blocks set in the brickwork. S. Swonnell & Sons went into voluntary liquidation in 1964, when competition from more modern and economic methods used elsewhere made their operation no longer viable. The practice of major brewing concerns to purchase their own malt business in order to secure their own raw materials supplies, and the capital backing these large enterprises invested in modern methods, inevitably brought the demise of under-capitalised family-owned malting businesses. Gooderham Investments Ltd, had the foresight to see the potential of these majestic commercial buildings, which the firm purchased in 1965, with work starting on converting the largest and newest malthouse which faced the saltings into the now world famous music concert hall and music school, which was formally opened by Her Majesty Queen Elizabeth II in 1967.

Where once the local fondly-named 'Snape Express' trundled sedately along its near straight branch line behind one of Holden's 6-coupled ex-Great Eastern tender engines, little now remains of this malt line. At the site of the Snape Junction, one can still see the railway boundary fence, curving away from the intact main line, the post and wire fence marking out the garden to a cottage beside the railway. The line passed through a shallow cutting then along hedgerows forming the fields, until it came to the River Alde; here may be discerned the short embankments either side, with the remains of the side timber stanchions visible above the waterline and the retaining brick abutments to the bridge. On the station side of the old bridge, the ballast formation is still intact and in good condition, as is the station master's house. Standing forlornly, and as if as a sentry standing guard over the last remains of this very special branch line, remarkably one may see an ex-GER 10-ton covered malt van of 1890 vintage. Double-spoked wheels, with hand-brake to one side only, external framing and corner plates gives its near century old age away. Alas, there are no remains of the railway lines to be discerned, although when lifted shortly after closure some of the chairs were dated 1880 with the bullhead rails of only 30ft length. Because of the near unspoilt condition of the buildings it is very easy to establish where all the sidings serving the malthouses were previously laid. A visit to Snape will be well rewarding to the railway enthusiast, the industrial archaeologist, the ornithologist and, of course, the music lover. A pleasant hour supping an ale in the Plough and Sail, so appropriately named, will soon conjure up the happy atmosphere which must have prevailed when farmers, maltsters, railwaymen and bargemen alike resorted to the tap room for a noggin or two!

16

Truman, Hanbury & Buxton
Black Eagle Brewery, Burton

The firm of Truman was founded in London in 1666, and with the development of the more go-ahead breweries, amalgamated with Hanbury and Buxton in the late 18th and 19th Centuries. The Burton brewery was built in 1873, sandwiched between the Midland Railway main line and the parallel Derby Road. The site was immediately opposite the largest Burton brewery on one site, that of Samuel Allsopp & Son.

The Derby Road brewery was developed over the years, but from its concept the plan of the brewery was built around the railway sidings which served it. A single-road locomotive shed was built into the western end of the main brewhouse block, with the records of the Midland Railway indicating that the brewery's own locomotive was handling the traffic from 1 July 1880.

Access to the brewery sidings was via a spur leading-

View of the 'Black Eagle' brewery taken from Horninglow Road, looking towards the Burton passenger station, with the coal yard sidings running parallel to the Truman, Hanbury & Buxton private sidings. (*IRS*).

off underneath a footbridge which passed over the Midland Railway main line, linking Derby Street East with Brook Street and Horninglow Street. The connecting siding passed through a gate and split into two sidings, which ran parallel to three Midland Railway storage sidings, divided by a 6ft high close-board fence. Two large malthouses at the western end were served by sidings and short run-round loops, with a second group of two sidings passing around the main brewhouse block, linking up by sharp curves at the eastern end throat, turning due-north into a single headshunt.

Right up to the early 1920s, most of the Black Eagle brewery's production was transported by the railway, hence the necessity for its own locomotives. The first to be supplied was from the Yorkshire Engineering Co in 1886, followed by a Hunslet in 1901, which was scrapped in 1954. In 1922, the first of three Peckett locomotives was delivered, all to that manufacturer's standard design for industrial 4-wheel saddle tanks.

Unlike most other breweries, Truman did not number

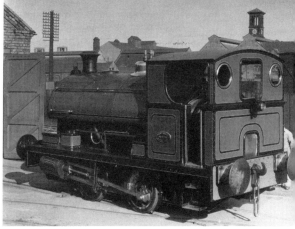

Truman's twin bulk beer rail tanker, built at Derby by British Railways in 1950 for the transport of beer between London and Burton. Similar traffic, though with different designs of tanks, was in use by A. Guinness and Ind Coope & Co Ltd. (*Crown Copyright, courtesy National Railway Museum*).

Immaculate Peckett & Sons Ltd 0–4–0ST, Works No 2136 in April 1958, outside Truman, Hanbury & Buxton's locomotive shed, with the sleeper fence dividing the private sidings from the British Railways tracks. Note the over-large buffer faces and large rear view aspect. (*R. C. Riley*).

its locomotives, nor specify a particular company livery, taking Peckett's standard mid-green and lining colour. During the 1955 railway strike Truman, like Bass and many other companies, had to make urgent provision for alternative road transport. This naturally speeded-up the transition to larger road tanker fleets and the gradual decline of 'beer by rail'. Due to the small volume of rail traffic, only one locomotive was in steam at any time, this working within the confines of the brewery network, except to take its wagons onto the transfer siding, which in turn served the main ex-Midland Railway goods yard and large coal sidings adjacent to the brewery.

In 1950, British Rail built at Derby a 4-wheel double tank wagon with 720-gallon demountable tanks, for transporting draught beer to be bottled at Truman's London Brewery. The Brick Lane brewery had a siding built by the Great Eastern Railway, authorised by an Act of Parliament in 1872 (35 Vic Ch XXIV).

With the modernisation and rationalisation of all breweries in the late 1960s, Truman decided to close down its Burton brewery and concentrate all production in London. The final closure of the Black Eagle Brewery, a notable landmark in Burton, was early in 1971, a sad day for all Burtonians.

A story which was related with some glee by other brewery employees, notably at Ind Coope, 'across the way', was the episode when one of Truman's cask number-takers who was fond of his beer, after a particularly heavy session one day decided to sleep it off in a railway van on the brewery sidings. Unfortunately he had misjudged his 'bedroom' and was rudely awakened in the sorting sidings at Dixie, several confused hours later, having been taken for a 'free' ride just down the line!

Truman, Hanbury & Buxton's 'Black Eagle' brewery layout remained unchanged until its closure in 1971. The locomotive shed was squeezed in at the end of the main brewhouse block which had a lengthy loading platform. (*Author*).

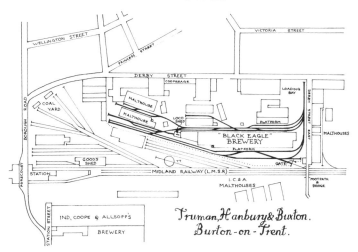

17

Warwicks & Richardsons Ltd, Newark, Notts

In the last century, Newark, known as the 'Metropolis of Malt', boasted eight or nine breweries, twenty malting companies, and twenty corn mills.

One of the earliest breweries was founded in 1766 by Samuel Sketchley, who left his native town of Burton-on-Trent to set up in business. He probably was prompted by the increasing competition in Burton, but as a professional brewer he was aware of the similarity of the water at Newark to that of his home town. No doubt his judgement was influenced by the geographical location of Newark, sited on the River Trent, with the Great North Road providing a transport interchange location. By 1794 Sketchley was in partnership with William Handley, brewing on land leased from the Duke of Newcastle at the Town Wharf; brewing continued from this site until the 1870s when the impending expiration of the lease, coupled with the restricted area available to cope with increasing trade, prompted the decision to move to larger premises. Ledger entries for the years 1794/6 include many local customers, but it is clear that 'Newark's Ales' were being distributed far and wide:

Thos. Wharton Esq., of Laurieston (Edinburgh) for sunday parcels of Ale.	£97.	18s.	2d.
Alex Gardner, Exchequer, Edinburgh, Sundry parcels of Ale.	£16.	15s.	1d.
Wm Boorman, Axe Inn, Aldermanbury, London December 8th 1795 – 14 half hds Ale 563 galls @ 16d	£37.	10s.	8d.
April 25th 1796 – 20 half hds Ale 808 galls @ 16d	£53.	17s.	4d.
T. Brocksop. Fore Street, London December 8th 1795 – 1 Hogshead Strong Ale 79 galls @ 20d	£6.	11s.	8d.

Road transport would have been nigh on impossible for long deliveries, even with the Great North Road, due to the unmade and very poor condition of the road surfaces. The beer would have been shipped to Hull by barge down the River Trent, and transferred into sea-going coastal tramp steamers to the ports of London and Edinburgh.

This beer traffic would have been balanced on the barges' return journeys up river with cargoes of Baltic oak, used for making the beer cask staves. William Handley's business interests not only included timber importing but also banking. The Warwick family, father and son both named Richard, had managed the Handley's banks in Newark and Sleaford. In 1856, the great-grandfather of the recently-retired chairman of Warwicks & Richardsons Ltd bought the run-down Handley brewery which was producing only 4,360 barrels annually, but which had been producing 7,500 barrels 60 years previously. Richard Warwick clearly recognised the full potential of Newark as an important transport centre and he later acquired a larger site alongside the navigable Trent, alongside which numerous maltings had and were being built, in order to make use of the water transport to the Humber ports.

This new brewery site in North Gate Road, close to the Great Northern Railway passenger and goods station, was opened in 1871, trading as Richard Warwick & Sons Ltd. On this site there already existed a small Grecian-style malting – fortunately this delightful building, which is of considerable architectural interest, remains intact. A 90ft deep well was sunk and produced an abundant supply of water, 15,000 gallons per hour, of a type well suited to brewing. Malt screens were installed by Robert Boby of Bury St. Edmunds, Suffolk, and further malthouses were at Cooks Lane and King Street, Balderton. As a progressive new brewery, the Company purchased a Merryweather steam fire engine, named *Gertrude*, which was able to draw water from the river, and to the great pride of employees was able to pump a jet of water over the full height of the 110ft brewery chimney! Six years after the opening, a further extension was built in 1877, with a suitably inscribed date stone. The very grand Victorian edifice on Northgate Road, which houses the unspoilt original 'open-plan' offices and screens, wall panelling and staircase, was built in 1882. Attention to detail is a joy to behold; even the cast-iron radiators were designed with castellated mouldings to harmonise with the town's castle! At this time there were 150 employees, of which 110 were employed in the brewery, with 18 horse drays delivering in the locality. With the purchase of the Trent Brewery (Richardson, Earp & Slater) in 1889, the company changed its name to Warwicks & Richardsons Ltd. During the next 30 years, three smaller breweries were brought under the wing of W. & R., namely McGeorge's, Heppenstall's and Davey's. By 1882, trade had dramatically increased with an annual production of 44,000 barrels, the only remaining local

(*opposite*) Numerous large maltings were served by wagon turntables, as was the brewery of Warwicks and Richardsons. (*By permission of the Controller, Ordnance Survey*).

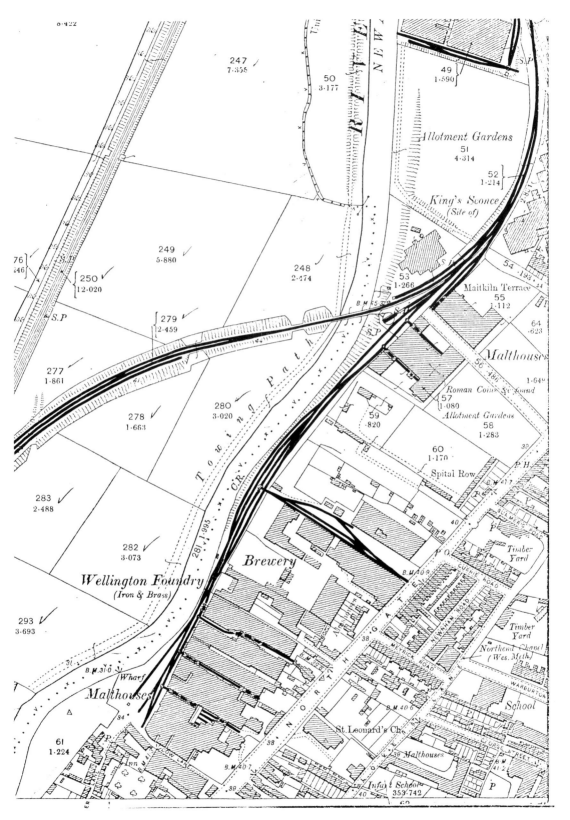

opposition being that of James Hole & Co Ltd. This brewery company had a large malting beside the Midland Railway station, close to the road bridge over the River Trent and opposite the large group of malthouses on the south side of the river. This large complex of malthouses which was part of Hole's brewing concern, consisted of six blocks, all fitted with R. Boby's milling machines; these buildings still exist, backing onto the river, but no longer with railway sidings serving them. James Hole & Co Ltd. also had further maltings at nearby Grantham.

By the turn of the century, annual output was 96,000 barrels, of which under half was within horse-delivery radius from Newark. The company had set up stores at Nottingham, Lincoln, Peterborough, Doncaster, Leicester, Sheffield, Derby, Newcastle, Manchester and Oakham. Most, if not all, were supplied by railway rather than the slower water transit.

The Trent valley first enjoyed railway communications with the opening of the Lincoln–Nottingham branch to Newark on 3 August 1846, engineered by George Stephenson. The line later became the Midland Railway, which was later to be challenged for its supremacy of rail transport in Newark. By an Act of Parliament the Great Northern Railway promoted a line to Marefield in 1872, taking over the local Newark & Leicester Railway. The London & North Western Railway Company joined with the GNR to extend the line south to Market Harborough, with the GNR line from Strathern to Melton opening on 30 June 1879. A price war with the Midland Railway began.

Both the GNR and MR double track main lines were on the flat valley bottom and crossed each other on a level diamond crossing, just north-east of the town of Newark. The Midland Railway station was sited just across the river opposite the castle with the usual railway hotel, The Midland, alongside the level-crossing. The Great Northern station was eventually to be the more important of the two, sited as it is on the eastern side of town near North Gate. A single line curved on a low embankment across the Trent valley connecting the MR line at its goods yard with the GNR, crossing over the canal by a skew bridge. On its construction in 1870 by the MR a series of spur sidings, loops and turntables was also installed, hugging the south bank of the river, the wagon turntables giving access into several maltings. These sidings swelled out into four loops in its centre, opposite the Warwicks & Richardsons brewery, which was also served by a wagon turntable. At the apex of the junction of the connecting line between the two main line companies and the spurs serving the maltings was sited a locomotive turntable, primarily for the use of MR 0–6–0 freight locomotives.

A letter of application by Messrs Warwick & Sons to the Midland Railway for a siding connection was approved by the General Manager's office at Derby on 5 October 1871. Further correspondence from the General Stores Department at Derby on 9 June 1873 listed the price of rails at £9 10s 0d (£9.50) per ton,

chairs at £6.00 per ton, spikes at £12.00 per ton, keys at £4.00 per 1000, and sleepers at 1/6d (7½p) each. 'Old points and crossings' were listed at £9 10s 0d per ton. Five years before the move to the North Gate Brewery, beer was being dispatched from the Town Wharf Brewery to the goods yards of the Midland Railway and Great Northern Railway.

By 1879 the company owned two coal wagons, carrying 1,478 tons 9 cwt between 1 April 1879 and 31 March 1880, but due to both having been damaged it was estimated that they would have carried a further 65 tons. Wagons Nos 3 and 4 were purchased from S. J. Claye, arriving at the brewery with coke from the Radford gasworks on 4 August 1881. No 3 was fitted with top rails for coke at a cost of £49, while No 4 without top rails cost just £46. In 1886 S. J. Claye's price for painting two coats, lettering and tarring inside a coal wagon was 17/6d (87½p) with wheels turned-up at a cost of £2 9s 8d (£2.48) which also included a 'thorough' repair. A fifth privately-owned coal wagon was in use by July 1897.

The use of horses gradually declined after the company purchased its first lorry in 1913, although this was commandeered by the War Office a year later! Foden's delivered two 6-wheel 12-ton undertype steam wagons in January 1931, with a third, 4-wheel 6-ton steam dray being delivered in July of the same year. Later, petrol lorries and eventually diesels (again from Foden) ousted the faithful heavy horses. With this gradual increase in road transport, rail-borne traffic started to decline. During the 1930s Warwicks & Richardsons supplied a Hull-based wines and spirits company, T. Linsley & Co Ltd, which owned 30 public houses and a larger number of off-licences, with about 250 barrels per week by rail. This was delivered by rail, but occasionally by barge down the navigable River Trent, until at the outbreak of World War II in 1939 an 8-wheel Foden diesel lorry took over the direct delivery. Beer was no longer delivered by rail wagons by 1946, although inward traffic of coal, coke, barley and hops was still being brought in by railway wagons. Warwicks & Richardsons coal wagons were only to be seen in the County of Nottingham, as they were used for the collection of coal and coke from local collieries. In 1956 British Railways was asked for a quotation to deliver a truck load of sweet stout to Gateshead but the cost was prohibitive, and there was no beer traffic from Newark under BR auspices.

Railway access into the Warwicks & Richardsons North Gate Brewery was via a wagon turntable situated on the second line of the four Midland sidings at the curve of the maltings spur line. The turntable spur crossed the inner line at right-angles and entered the brewery precincts via a gate, whereupon a turnout followed quickly by a second, forming two loops. The first building on the right served by the long straight siding was the original malthouse built in 1864, which has a single lucam overhanging the railway track to facilitate hauling sacks of barley to the top floor. Two-thirds of the way down the rectangular yard was sited a

complex 'scissors' pointwork which brought together the three sidings into one short headshunt, which terminated beside the road entrance gates from North Gate Road. In 1908 a long straight loading bank was built as part of a large bottling stores. This was the last major structural development. A further siding to serve this loading bank was put in at the time of construction; it becoming almost as important as the bank opposite from which the casks of draught beer were dispatched.

The draught beer loading bank is arcaded, with fine quality brickwork arches forming covered working areas, more normally accommodated by corrugated-iron sheet canopies in other breweries and maltings. Towards the centre of the brewery yard is situated the boiler house with the coal bunkers, which usually had three or four of the company's coal wagons discharging into them at any one time. Although line drawings and advertising posters showed GNR locomotives within the brewery curtilage this was not so, as horses stabled at Northgate station carried out all internal shunting. The sidings remained in use until the early 1950s, mainly for the delivery of coal for the brewhouse boilers which were converted to oil-firing in the mid-1950s, thereby reducing rail traffic to intermittent bottling stores and general brewing materials. Most of the sidings were removed, although even to this day the main straight siding running the full length of the brewery yard, and one loop siding, are still visible, passing the listed buildings of the malthouse and

Rake of two Great Western and four Midland Railway vans at the bottling stores bank, taken in 1910. (*Major F. R. Warwick*).

brewhouse complex. Nothing now remains of the previously hectic Midland Railway sidings alongside the river bank which served the many malthouses on either side of the brewery, nature having taken back its own. The wagon turntable, which the brewery was responsible for maintaining and cleaning out its sump, is now but a memory of those who had to strain to turn the 10ton railway wagons into the brewery. A metal gate long since padlocked bars the way into the brewery from the old main line sidings.

In 1962 Warwicks and Richardsons Ltd was bought-out by John Smith of Tadcaster. Ironically, the last remaining opposing brewery in Newark, James Hole & Co, became fellow bed-mates, as it had been acquired by Courage a year or two earlier, Courage finally acquiring the Yorkshire brewery of John Smith in 1970. The North Gate Brewery finally ceased brewing in 1966, but has since been in use as offices and transport depot, the site now undergoing restoration, a great credit to the Courage Group for preserving such a delightful gem of Victorian industrial architecture. The grand tradition of brewing in Newark fortunately continues at J. Hole's Castle Brewery, near the centre of town, its fine façade competing for grandeur with that of Warwicks & Richardsons Ltd in North Gate.

18

Wrexham Lager Beer Company Ltd, North Wales

In the rolling hills of North Wales, several German immigrants built a brewery on the design and principle of their Bavarian homeland. That was back in 1882, when it was unique as the first lager brewery in this country.

Wrexham was selected because of the quality of its water, highly suitable for the production of the unique Continental lager, at that time a dark Munich type. For easy transport, the Great Central Railway served the town. Nearby in the Shrewsbury area high quality barley is grown. So it was that the brewery was built on the established lager brewery principles. However, a most important aspect of lager brewing is the storage of the lager under cooled conditions. Caves were excavated under the hills for this purpose, but unlike the Continental practice of cutting ice from rivers and ponds to keep the product cool, the British weather was not so dependable. Wrexham Brewery thus was also the first in the country to have installed a mechanical refrigeration system.

One of the directors, Ivan Levenstein, was travelling on a train when he met Robert Graesser. Their talk turned to the new brewery, and by the end of the journey Mr Graesser had bought a majority shareholding. He quickly appraised the merits of this lager brewery, and extended its range of original dark Bavarian lager by adding a light lager and one of a

Pilsner style. In spite of his efforts, there was still a resistance in the home market which was imbued with traditional ale drinking.

Robert Graesser took with him on his voyage to the United States in 1904 on the White liner *Baltic* a cask of Wrexham draught lager, this being the first occasion that a British liner carried draught beer. It travelled well and served in perfect condition, so that it was not long before Wrexham Lager was being supplied to several shipping lines, such as Cunard and Elder Dempster. During the winter big supplies of lager were sent to Liverpool by road transport, in the early days by steam wagon. The beer for Southampton docks was loaded onto rail wagons, with complete goods trains being specially arranged to take the Wrexham Lager for the three-month cruises of such ships as the *Caronia* and *Mauretania*. These trains carried up to 1,800 casks of five gallon capacity each, in twelve covered vans. The casks were packed with blocks of ice to keep the beer cool and in good condition while in transit. These vans were marshalled by the shire horse who pulled them out of the brewery sidings onto the exchange siding during the late afternoon. A Great Western locomotive then assembled them into a mixed freight train if there were only a few — if there was a large consignment for a special sailing then the beer train would leave in the early evening for its journey south. The fame of

Inner yard scene at Wrexham Lager Beer Works *circa* 1922. The arch to the right-hand siding had a wagon turntable which served a spur to the right, handling spent grains and coal. (*Wrexham Lager Brewery Co*).

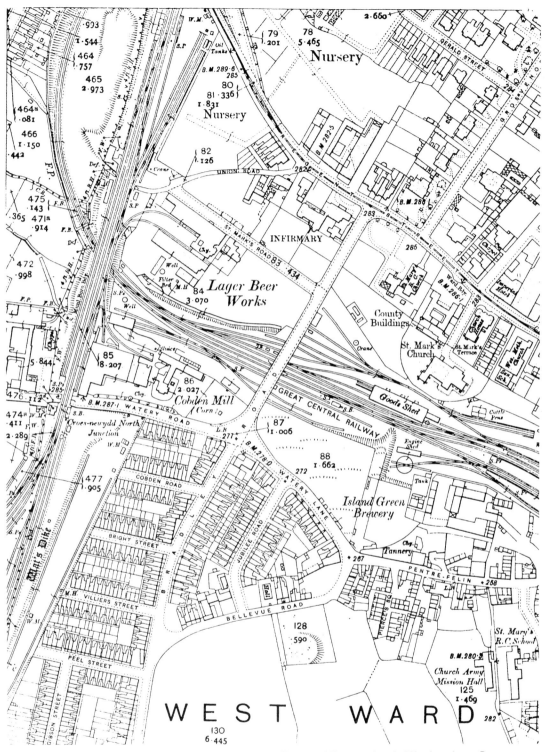

The two sidings serving the Wrexham Lager Brewery were extended in the 1930s to include a wagon turntable and a high-level spur. *By permission of the Controller, Ordnance Survey).*

Great Western Railway 2–6–0 No 8341 waiting to pull away with its load of twelve beer vans on 27 June 1931, destined for Southampton Docks. (*Wrexham Lager Brewery Co*).

Wrexham Lager was by then spreading around the world, the ships not just carrying draught but also bottled beer. Many clubs and famous hotels were also selling these lagers, including the Great Western Hotel, Carlton Club, and the Constitutional Club.

A fascinating letter is treasured by the brewery, which well illustrates how far afield its products were to be found. When Lord Kitchener relieved Khartoum in 1898, a stock of bottled Wrexham lager with its Ace of Clubs trade mark was found. The letter dated 5 October 1898, from a staff sergeant major in the Army Service Corps reads:

> Gentleman, I enclose herewith one of your labels which was taken off a bottle found in the grounds of Gordon's Palace at Khartoum on the 3d September 1898. I send it as a matter of curiosity, just to let you know how far your Wrexham Lager Beer can be had.

In 1922, it became easier to buy Wrexham lager in the town in which it is brewed, when the Cross Foxes Hotel was purchased, followed in September 1938 with a further 23 public houses bought from the local brewery, Beirnes, which closed down after going into liquidation.

Sometime in the late 1930s the GWR engaged a Mr Setterfield who had been the catering superintendent on the Cunard shipping line. His goodwill typified the excellent trade relationships which the Wrexham Lager Beer Company enjoyed. He was so keen on the lager that he virtually gave all the business on the GWR trains hotels and refreshment rooms to the Wrexham Lager Brewery. He even produced a deep green ash tray, which had 'GWR' printed on the lip and 'Wrexham Lager' on the base with the Ace of Clubs in the middle – an early forerunner of dual advertising. This was virtually the only lager served in the GWR trains, and stocks were held at Snow Hill station

(Birmingham), Cardiff, Bristol, Exeter and Paddington. Large quantities were loaded onto passenger trains at Wrexham station for the Birkenhead–Paddington services route. Draught Wrexham was on sale at the large hotels at all the major railway stations.

The brewery was built with two short rail sidings, including one at the second floor which served the spent grains shutes. Entry to this siding was via a turntable giving access into the inner high-level yard, through the central boiler house building. Below this spent grain spur siding was sited the stables for the local horse transport. It is recorded that the Wrexham Lager Beer Co Ltd had at least one of their own 5-plank open wagons, used primarily for the spent grains traffic. All shunting within the brewery was done by heavy horses, two being needed to move a fully loaded van. Access into the brewery by rail was from the high-level line, with a long siding which was shared with the Cobden Corn Mill on the opposite side of the low-level goods yard. Adjacent to the brewery were several sidings at the high-level, where no doubt the covered vans of lager were assembled to form the occasional complete trains of beer. Due to the limitations of the brewery's two curved sidings, storage of empty and full vans on their way to customers was in the exchange sidings. Of the several other breweries in the town, in the 1920s including the Island Green Brewery and the Cambrian Brewery, none was directly served by its own private rail sidings. In the rebuilding of the brewery in the early 1950s, the rail sidings were removed. As with many country towns, breweries have successively closed down; with a brewing town such as Wrexham, this has been even more poignant. As late as the 1880s nineteen breweries were listed in the town, and six independent malt houses. Today Wrexham boasts only two, the Border Breweries in Tuttle Street and the Wrexham Lager Beer Company Ltd in Central Road. The country's first all-lager brewery is still going strong, and exporting all round the world.

The Little Pilsen lager brewery was re-invigorated by its incorporation within the Ind Coope group in 1949.

19
Worthington & Co Ltd, High Street, Burton

Worthington claims the distinction of being the oldest surviving brewery in Burton, William Worthington having established his brewery on the east side of the High Street in 1761. Over successive years several smaller breweries were absorbed, including Evans, Dodson and J. W. Wilson, all of the High Street.

William, junior, married into the Evans family in 1791, and when William Worthington, senior, died in 1800 he was able to leave his family two breweries. Henry Evans was a successful common brewer, merchant and gentleman, who also had a large interest in the Burton Boat Company and the corn mill. He owned a 40-ton barge which carried beer, iron to the local foundries, and timber brought in from the Baltic ports up the River Trent to Gainsborough. By 1790 he had become one of the wealthiest and influential people in the town.

Loading ale onto railway wagons commenced on 30 September 1863, with records of the Midland Railway goods agent indicating that Worthington's first locomotive was in use from 19 November 1872. This would appear to conflict with the first known record of Hudswell Clarke 0–4–0 saddle tank No 262 having been delivered in 1883. It may well have been that this first locomotive referred to was in fact a locally-made Thornewill & Warham well tank. Early records of this

manufacturer are scant, although it is known it supplied 66 brewery locomotives! Five miles of private railway sidings belonged to the Worthington brewery, in the halcyon days an average 200 barrels on rail trucks leaving on the Great Northern, Midland, London & North Western and North Staffordshire Railways. The highest despatch of barrels was 2,000 in one day.

Since 1895 Worthington locomotives worked trains between some old maltings previously owned by the Burton Brewery Company, on what was known as the Sanders branch of the Midland Railway, at a fee of £40 per annum.

The Station Street brewery was connected to the Hay Branch by a level-crossing over the High Street in 1863. Traffic up to the Dixie exchange sidings was originally worked by horses along the Guild Street branch until the end of 1864, when the High Street branch was opened throughout. The stone arch Trent Bridge had to be rebuilt to allow clear headroom for the standard loading gauge line to pass underneath. Thereafter

A commercial postcard of the early 1900 period, showing a composite scene which indicates the true brewery transport scene. Midland Railway open wagons are being shunted by Worthington's beautiful royal blue-and red lined livery 0–4–0 saddle tank, with the two shunters in the foreground. (*IRS*).

Worthington No 1 propels a steel wagon away from Worthington's Brewery built in 1880. A petrol-engine shunter with a rake of wagons loads at the platform. (R. C. Riley).

Midland Railway tank locomotives hauled Worthington's traffic via Wetmore Road and Hawkins Lane. In 1882 the Station Street level-crossing was opened, giving connection with the brewery to the new cooperage and cask-washing plant, and thence via Robinson's branch to Bond End branch with access to Shobnall and the Crown Maltings. This was later to be considerable benefit to the amalgamated companies of Bass/Worthington, which joined forces in 1926. Prior to this merger, Worthington had taken-over another, the Burton Brewery Company in 1914.

The Burton Brewery Company had its own siding with ale loading, starting on 3 February 1863, from the High Street. The firm acquired its first locomotive, again believed to be by Thornewill & Warham, on 3 October, 1867. A second was in use from 3 September 1872; this company evidently believed that so far as its railway operation was concerned, three was the lucky number. When Worthington took over the Burton Brewery Company, it inherited the third Burton Brewery Company locomotive, a Manning Wardle built in 1899. This was rebuilt two years after the amalgamation and sold in 1923.

Worthington owned a total of ten steam locomotives, 4-wheel saddle tanks, between the years 1883 to 1945 when the last, a Bagnall, was delivered. Unlike the other major breweries, Worthington's had a considerable fleet of petrol engine shunters. The first two were delivered in 1924, manufactured by Honeywill Bros; these were soon followed by one more in the next two years. The previous policy of buying from this manufacturer was changed several years later, as two Planets were purchased from F. C. Hibberd of London, between 1929 and 1934. All these petrol engine locomotives were converted to diesel between 1950 and 1957. The livery was an attractive mid-blue with scarlet double coach lining. On the amalgamation with Bass, Ratcliffe & Gratton in 1926, in order not to duplicate numbers in both companies' considerable fleet of locomotives, the Worthington locomotives were renumbered in 1960. They continued to retain their blue livery, instead of adopting Bass turkey red.

Hudswell Clarke 0–4–0T, Works No 1417, built in 1920 for Worthington & Co, looking resplendent in its blue lined-red livery, on 12 April, 1958. (R. C. Riley).

20

Specialised Brewery and Malting Trade Rolling Stock

Privately-owned freight wagons were in use by several breweries from an early date, the earliest probably being about 1860.

During the 1850s major improvements in the design of wagons took place. Previously wagons were all timber, with wooden solebars and dumb buffers. With the improvements came sprung buffers, axleboxes, and 3-link spring couplings. Wheels and eliptical springing improved the designs, which now had some form of standardisation. Wagon loads improved from the early days of six tons, so that by the late 1860s loads rapidly increased successively from 7, 8 and 10 to 12 tons. These latter two became the normal load right up to the 1970s, when came the introduction of the bulk wagons of British Rail. Within the general improvements, probably the most important was the braking system. Early wheels were open-spoked and were in use on privately-owned wagons up to 1939. The earliest wagons often had no brakes – the first type fitted were large wooden blocks worked by a lever on a fulcrum fitted just above the brake block on one wheel only; some models had the two wheels on one side only braked, with later improvements being made by replacing the wood blocks with cast-iron. It will be well appreciated the problems that this one-sided braking must have caused with railwaymen taking many severe risks in crawling between wagons and running-round to get at the brake levers. In 1911 the Board of Trade drew up regulations regarding the fitting of brakes with which all privately-owned wagons were required to conform. Due to the advent of World War I, this was delayed until registration and standardisation was introduced in 1923, under the Railway Clearing House scheme. Earlier Railway Clearing House specifications had been drawn-up in 1887 and 1909, but the final 1923 design was perpetuated for 12-ton open wagons by the LMS and LNER. The overall dimensions for both 7-plank and 8-plank wagons was 16ft 6in over headstocks, body width 8ft 0in, wheelbase 9ft 0in, and 3ft 1in wheels.

The insides of mineral wagons was normally painted a light brown, or coated with bitumen in coal traffic wagons. The outside was a different matter altogether! The first known examples of private-owner wagons displaying their names were built about 1860. Not only was the owner's name proudly displayed, but in the case of the vast majority of wagons owned by collieries and coal merchants, many other details were included. In all cases the load and tare weights were indicated. It was not long before many vehicles began to display advertising slogans and often forms of company logo or emblem. Brewers were quick to seize this opportunity to sell their products and several very ornate early examples are illustrated. Many of these were works of art both in concept, design and execution. As far as covered vans were concerned, the early principles seemed to be 'cover every square inch'. From the early examples prior to 1900, with their detailed information, styles changed towards more simple and bold lettering.

It is interesting to note the various vehicles within one of the breweries, Bass, in 1887, when 40,000 tons of coal, and 2,000 tons of coke were used. In that year there were 2,580 employees and 150 horses, 35 wagons, 38 carts, 75 floaters, 2 drays and 110 railway wagons. In addition to those privately-owned wagons, the pre-grouping railway companies' wagons were also in general use and could be seen in all the brewery sidings.

The types of private wagons used, both open and closed, were originally those of the main line railway companies, particularly of the Midland Railway. Later as the brewery companies became more discerning in their requirements, so special vans were brought into use. So far as the raw materials were concerned, barley or malt was chiefly transported in sacks in closed vans.

Rare example of an 8-ton van built at the end of the last century for this small Kentish family brewery company, which is still in existence. Livery is light cream with dark blue lettering shaded yellow; white roof and wheel rims with black ironwork. (*HMRS Hurst Nelson Collection*).

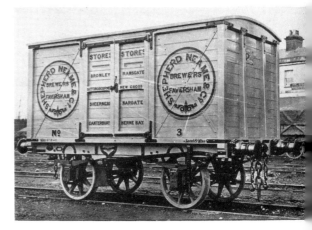

Due to the extent of man-handling and the ever-increasing manpower costs, ways and means were looked into to provide bulk grain transport. Thus the 20-ton bulk grain van became a familiar wagon used at breweries and spirit distilleries. These wagons worked between the areas where maltings were most numerous, such as East Anglia and brewing centres, chiefly London and Burton. Many designs were used, but all on the same principle of top loading, usually two flat sliding hatches, and bottom discharge between the rails. These familiar vans were also privately owned, particularly by Bass and later Bass/Charrington, with appropriate company lettering. It was the practice of Ind Coope to use railway company rolling stock, but with the addition of a 'Fablon' self-adhesive poster which incorporated the red-and-black 'Hand' logo at the top, surmounting a white oval with grey block letters 'Bulk Grain'. Below this, in black lettering on a mid-grey background, was 'For Ind Coope, Burton-on-Trent'. This measured 2ft 0in x 3ft 0in and was fixed to each wagon on a central panel, one to each side. The earliest livery for bulk grain vans was mid-grey, but in later BR days bauxite was used, giving way in the 1980s to the mid-green used in the 50-ton Polybulk bogie containers. Various modifications took place over the years, with both 'Oleo' and 'Dowty' hydraulic buffers in use. Axleboxes also varied, from 'Hybox' to roller bearings. Control for the bottom discharge was by either one or two side fitted wheels at the cambered chutes. At each end, a vertical ladder gave access to the flat top, which usually had a walkway allowing operatives to direct the filling chutes from the grain silos into the top hatches. It was essential to ensure that these hatches were water-tight, and it was common practice to have a tarpaulin sheet over the top.

Brewery-owned 7-plank and 8-plank wagons were used chiefly by the medium sized companies for coal as inward traffic, with ash and spent grain outward. Because of the much greater volumes involved with the large companies, it was more economical to use colliery-owned coal wagons.

As with the thinking towards bulk handling of grain, the same applied to the bulk transit of draught beer in tanks. It was Allsopp which led the field in this respect, commencing in the mid 1930s with 11-ton rail tank wagons for the draught lager traffic from Alloa in Scotland to the bottling stores at Burton. There were several variations of patterns from Charles Roberts & Co Ltd of Wakefield, but the most distinctive feature of these was their filler domes.

Two designs incorporated three squat domes. Liveries varied from 'Graham's Golden Lager' to 'Allsopp's Lager' with Ind Coope & Allsopp in white letters on black and vice-versa. Most of the rail tank wagons had the vehicle number painted on each barrel end. The tanks were glass-lined and in two or three compartments, which were required to be either full or all empty. Most of these tank wagons were fully fitted for fast train operation. The typical dimension was 10ft 0in wheelbase with a tank of 15ft 4in long by 6ft 4¾in diameter. Several were built at Derby between 1939 and 1947.

The loading of beer wagons, vans, open trucks or tanks, or the unloading of bulk grain vans, was carried out at each brewery by its own staff. At every location loading banks were to be seen, many with inset rails forming roller-ways for the casks of beer. The loaders used a 'bobbing-stick' which they deftly used to push and guide the casks of beer up into the wagons, only touching the casks with their hands when inside the rail wagon. In 1965 the London Midland Region introduced long-wheelbase wagons for use with palletised cask handling, but although this considerabley speeded-up the loading of wagons, it nevertheless came too late to save the rail beer trade. A 20-ton covered wagon could take 20 hogsheads, (54 gallons each) while an open wagon could take 60 firkins (9 gallons each).

To give some idea of the volume of traffic handled by Burton in a week in the early 1960s, it is interesting to note that of 3,770 wagons forwarded from Burton, 1,522 were of beer, 2166 were general merchandise, and only 82 coal and minerals. About half of the beer wagons used at this time were of the shock-absorbing type. With the introduction of the palletised ale wagons, British Rail also introduced de-mountable tanks, which

The Felinfoel Brewery's coal wagon built in 1900 standing outside the Gloucester Railway Carriage & Wagon Company's works. Livery black with white lettering. (*Courtesy National Railway Museum*).

A 12-ton beer van built in 1929 for the LMS. It is painted in a light grey livery with white lettering, black solebar, wheels and brake gear. Note ventilation gaps between each plank. (*Courtesy National Railway Museum*).

held 1,080 gallons. These were painted in the liveries of the breweries which used them, chiefly for the Irish trade via Heysham and Holyhead, also Continental traffic via Harwich. The Channel Islands trade also used these tanks.

Because of the seasonal nature of the raw materials – namely malt and hops – traffic at Burton was subjected to considerable fluctuations. Within this period of the early 1960s, some 70,000 tons of barley were handled by the Burton breweries, most of this coming from the Eastern Counties. Several thousand tons of this barley when malted was forwarded to Alloa Brewery in Scotland by Ind Coope. In return, a considerable tank wagon traffic of lager came to Burton for bottling. Because of its very perishable nature, this beer had to be delivered to the bottling stores the next day, the checking of the manifest being of the utmost importance to ensure the correct and rapid distribution of each wagon. Of a very much lesser volume and importance of traffic was the spent grain and hops which were used for the manufacture of animal feed because of the high protein content. There was also some limited traffic in yeast, as there was always an excess due to its rapid expansion, this material being used in the food and medicinal manufacturing. Because of the high esteem in which the Burton water was held, this too was transported by rail. A well situated on the corner of Shobnall Street and Shobnall Road was the site of the exported water to Magee Marshall's brewery in Bolton. Special covered vans were used for this traffic, which was of limited volume and duration at the time of the maximum 'beer trade', around 1925.

There are two very sound reasons why private wagons were used. Firstly, there was value of good

British Railways 6-wheel road/rail tank trailer truck, Diagram DD9, built in 1951. The two types of road tankers were built by Dyson's. (A. Guinness & Son).

personalised company advertising in the form of the elaborate and decorative signwriting. Secondly, private wagons could be held at sidings as long as they were required, without having to pay demurrage charges which were required when railway company wagons were utilised. All vehicles were required to pay a shunting fee, which amounted to 6d (2½p) per day in 1925. Many vans were often seen on sidings for a very long time, practically becoming mobile warehouses. The outbreak of World War II in 1939 really began the decline of the private-owner wagon, with only a few being constructed during the war years. The majority of wagons were pooled at the outbreak of war, allowing them to be used throughout the country, and cutting-out very wasteful marshalling and returning to owners, often without loads. Although the breweries were large consumers of coal, very few used open wagons in their own liveries for this purpose. This is understandable because all collieries had their own, and these amounted to 85% of all privately-owned wagons in 1918, when a census was taken. Various collieries specialised in the market place for their own special types of coal and the brewing industry, including malting and hop drying, received notable attention on several collieries' wagons.

Between 1939 and 1946, some fifteen 4-wheel road/rail beer tank wagons were constructed, five at Derby and ten at Wolverton. These had 10ft 0in wheelbase standard steel underframes, with fully-fitted handbrakes of the double-shoe Morton type. The tops

North British Railway yeast traffic van, built in 1903. Note the ventilation louvres to sides and ends. (*National Railway Museum*).

of the underframes were steel decked, painted in Bauxite brown. Hinged flaps at each end could be extended flat over the buffers in order to allow the pneumatic tyres of the road trailers to pass over from end-loading docks. Chains with turnbuckles secured the tanker at eight fixing points, four to each side, which normally fitted two points on each side of the road tanker. Broad plates ran the full length to guide and control lateral movement of the road wheels. The load indicated was 10 tons and these wagons were used primarily by Whitbread. A 6-wheeled version was in use on the Great Western Railway, later the Western Region of British Railways, specifically for the Guinness traffic from the Park Royal Brewery in North London. The load for these was 14 tons, on account of the additional centre wheels which were not braked. All were marked 'Shunt with care'.

Both the North British Railway and the Glasgow & South Western Railway used open slat high-sided wagons for cask beer transit. These came into use in the 1890s and were of several designs, with loads varying between 10 and 12 tons in both short and long wheelbase forms. In the early designs braking was on one wheel only, often operated by the most simple of fulcrum principles. The livery was invariably mid-grey with white lettering which indicated that the traffic conveyed was 'Empty Casks', and the destination to which the vehicles was to be returned. Door opening which was central and double-doored, was of hinged and sliding type. To brace the high sides, four top cross-braces were fitted. Many of these wagons passed into LNER hands and were to be seen in its old Northern area.

Yeast vans were provided for this very limited type of traffic by the Great Eastern, the Midland and the North British railway companies. These were built in the early 1900s, only a few being constructed. They were fully-fitted and well ventilated – the Midland Railway type resembled a cattle wagon. The North British type had small slots in two panels of three to each side and at each end, to the lower waist area, the side sheets being of tongue-and-groove vertical boards. Railway

companies painted these wagons in grey, with white lettering.

The railways did not have universal approval from all brewers, as is illustrated by a report to the board of directors of Boddington's Strangeways Brewery Manchester, by Henry Boddington II in 1882. He was an ardent promoter of the Manchester Ship Canal and subscribed considerable time and money to its inception. He clearly disliked travel by rail, and supplied the following 'proof' in support of the canal scheme:

My firm paid for Railway Carriage at the Manchester Brewery last year – £4,318.13.8d. I believe the Canal would conduce to a large saving in this total sum.

My firm paid for raw materials at the Manchester Brewery last year.		
	Malt	£36,124. 8.3
	Hops	£ 5,933.15.9
	Sugar	£ 6,084. 1.8
	Corn	£ 1,526. 5.1
	Hay	£ 446. 2.3
	Coal	£ 940. 1.3
	Isinglas etc	£ 802.17.0
	Staves	£ 328. 9.3
	Hoops	£ 131. 7.6
		£52,317. 8.0

I believe the Canal would effect a considerable saving in the prime cost of the raw materials we use by bringing the market nearer to us.
I am convinced that the Canal would be a great outlet and aid the extension of our trade.

The Railway rate to Barrow is 17s 6d.	
viz For the full 36 gallon barrel, 4 cwt	3s 6d
For the empty 36 gallon barrel, 1 cwt	8d
Making together	4s 2d

Taking 36s as the average net selling price to the dealer, 4s 2d is a tax of 11.57 per cent on the cost.
We gave up our Agency in Barrow chiefly because of the heavy railway rate, which did not allow us to compete with other Brewers with a profit to ourselves. We could send beer by water for nearly half the rate. I believe the Canal would be of immense benefit to the Trade of Manchester.

Works No.	Date Built	Type	Cylinders/ horsepower	Builder	Brewery number/name	Notes
S. ALLSOPP & SONS LTD, BURTON (Amalgamated with Ind Coope Ltd, June 1934)						
60	1862	0-4-0ST	14in x 20in o/c	Manning Wardle	1 'Leeds'	Sold to North of England Industrial Iron & Coal Ltd, Middlesborough. 3ft 6in wheels.
75	1866	0-4-0ST	14in x 20in o/c	Hudswell, Clarke & Rodgers	2	
148	1874	0-4-0ST	14in x 20in o/c	Hudswell, Clarke & Rodgers	3	Rebuilt by Hawthorn Leslie in 1912. Sold to Redbourn Hill Iron & Coal Co. Scunthorpe. 3ft 6in wheels.
168	1875	0-4-0ST	14in x 20in o/c	Hudswell, Clarke & Rodgers	4	Scrapped in 1920. 3ft 6in wheels.
177	1876	0-4-0ST	14in x 20in o/c	Hudswell, Clarke & Rodgers	5	Rebuilt by Hawthorne Leslie 1912. Scrapped in 1922. 3ft 6in wheels.
178	1876	0-4-0ST	14in x 20in o/c	Hudswell, Clarke & Rodgers	6	Rebuilt by Thornewill & Warham in 1901. Scrapped in 1934. 3ft 6in wheels.
647	1903	0-4-0ST	15in x 22in o/c	Hudswell Clarke	7	Scrapped in 1926. 3ft 7in wheels.
1858	1925	0-4-0ST		Andrew Barclay	8	Scrapped in 1954. Absorbed into Ind Coope & Allsopp.
393	1874	0-4-0WT	12in x 18in o/c	Thornewill & Warham	4	Scrapped in 1926. Ex Bass, Ratcliff & Gretton, sold in 1917 to Holwell Iron Co. Ltd. Melton Mowbray. 3ft 6in wheels. Repaired by Hudswell Clarke.
Livery:- Dark green with orange coach lining. Large brass oval company nameplates incorporating hand motif with red background.						
BASS, RATCLIFF & GRETTON LTD, BURTON						
--	1863	0-4-0T	14in x 20in o/c	Thornewill & Warham		Square-top tank.
224	1863	0-4-0WT	14in x 20in o/c	Thornewill & Warham		This locomotive is depicted on the pictorial swing sign of the Locomotive Inn, Burton-on-Trent.
249	1865	0-4-0WT	14in x 20in o/c	Thornewill & Warham	1	Sold in 1876.
259	1865	0-4-0WT	14in x 20in o/c	Thornewill & Warham	2	Sold in 1880.
303	1869	0-4-0WT	14in x 20in o/c	Thornewill & Warham	3	Out of service 1891 to 1901.
353	1872	0-4-0WT	14in x 20in o/c	Thornewill & Warham	4	Rebuilt in 1898, Sold in 1913.
373	1983	0-4-0WT	14in x 20in o/c	Thornewill & Warham	5	To WD at Purfleet in May 1917.
393	1984	0-4-0WT	14in x 20in o/c	Thornewill & Warham	6	Rebuilt in 1900 by Hunslet Engineering Co. Ltd. as saddle tank. Sold in 1917 to S. Allsopp & Son.
400	1875	0-4-0WT	14in x 20in o/c	Thornewill & Warham	7	Rebuilt in 1899 by Hunslet Engineering Co.Ltd. as saddle tank. Sold in 1903. To WD at Purfleet in May 1917.
420	1876	0-4-0WT	14in x 20in o/c	Thornewill & Warham	8	Rebuilt in 1898 by Hunslet Engineering Co.Ltd. as saddle tank. Sold in 1917.
	1876	0-4-0WTG	14in x 20in o/c	Thornewill & Warham	1	Sold in 1900.
425	1877	0-4-0WT	14in x 20in o/c	Thornewill & Warham	9	Sold in 1901.
455	1880	0-4-0ST	14in x 21in o/c	Thornewill & Warham	2	Sold in 1906.
609	1891	0-4-0ST	14in x 21in o/c	Thornewill & Warham	3	Rebuilt in 1904, Sold in 1963.
5567	1899	0-4-0ST	14in x 21in o/c	Neilson Reid	10	Sold in 1963. Weight 23½ tons.
5568	1899	0-4-0ST	14in x 21in o/c	Neilson Reid	11	Sold in 1964. Weight 23½ tons.
5759	1900	0-4-0ST	14in x 21in o/c	Neilson Reid	1	Sold in 1963. Weight 23½ tons.
5760	1900	0-4-0ST	14in x 20in o/c	Neilson Reid	2	Weight 22¼ tons.
5907	1901	0-4-0ST	14in x 21in o/c	Neilson Reid	9	This locomotive hauled saloon for King Edward VIII on 22 May 1902. Both preserved at the Bass Museum, Burton.
19848	1913	0-4-0ST	14in x 21in	North British Locomotive Co	4	Sold in 1964. Weight 23½ tons.
3027	1939	0-4-0D	Gardener 4 cylinder 85hp	E. E. Baguley	5	Sold in 1967. Weight 15 tons.
416566	1957	0-4-0D	4 cylinder 88hp	Ruston & Hornsby	8	Sold in 1968.
3509	1958	0-4-0D	Gardener 8 cylinder 204hp	E. E. Baguley	6	Sold in 1969. Weight 32 tons.
10003	1960	0-4-0TG	Rolls Royce 6 cylinder 207hp	Sentinel	12	Sold in 1969.
3568	1962	0-4-0D	Gardener 8 cylinder 204hp	E. E. Baguley	1	Sold in 1968. Weight 32 tons.
10085	1961	0-4-0TG	Rolls Royce 6 cylinder 207hp	Sentinel	7	
3589	1962	0-4-0D	Gardener 4 cylinder 110hp	E. E. Baguley	4	Sold in 1967. Weight 20 tons.
3590	1962	0-4-0D	Gardener 4 cylinder 110hp	E. E. Baguley	11	Sold in 1968. Weight 20 tons.
BURTON BREWERY CO LTD (Premises acquired by Ind Coope & Co Ltd in 1927)						
228	1867	0-4-0ST	o/c	Manning Wardle	1	
	1872	0-4-0ST	o/c	Manning Wardle	2	
593	1877	0-4-0ST	o/c	Manning Wardle	3	Sold to J. D. Nowell & Son, Warrington.
1427	1899	0-4-0ST	o/c	Manning Wardle	4	Sold to Worthington & Co. Ltd, Burton in 1916.
CHARRINGTON & CO, BURTON						
276	1885	0-4-0ST	12in x 18in o/c	Hudswell Clarke	-	Sold to Rossett Sand & Gravel Ltd, Flintshire. Rebuilt 1922.
1437	1921	0-4-0ST	15in x 22in o/c	Hudswell Clarke	-	Sold to J.Crosfield & Sons Ltd, Warrington. 3ft 4in wheels.
A. GUINNESS & SON, ST JAMES GATE, DUBLIN (Narrow gauge 1ft 10in) Closed in 1957						
2477	1875	0-4-0		Sharp, Stewart & Co		Withdrawn 1913. Weight 2 tons.
	1877	0-4-0WTG	1 x 6½in x 8in ov single	T. Lewin & Co	2/Hops'	Withdrawn 1914. 140lb/sq in. Cost £366. Weight 5 tons.
	1877	0-4-0WTG	1 x 6½in x 8in ov single	T. Lewin & Co	3/Malt'	Withdrawn 1927. 140lb/sq in. Cost £366. Weight 5 tons.
2764	1878	0-4-0T		Sharp, Stewart & Co	4	Withdrawn 1925. Outside Stephenson valve year. Weight 6 tons. Cost £597.
2765	1878	0-4-0T		Sharp, Stewart & Co	5	Withdrawn 1925. Outside Stephenson valve year. Weight 6 tons. Cost £597.

Works No.	Date	Type	Cylinders/horsepower	Builder	Brewery number/name	Notes
1337	1882	0-4-0T	7in x 8½in	Avonside Engine Co	6	Withdrawn in 1936. Weight 7.4 tons. Scrapped in 1947.
	1887	0-4-0T		W. Spence	7	No. 7 & 8 withdrawn in 1948; Nos 9, 10 & 11 in 1949; Nos 14, 16, 18 & 19 in 1951; No 12 in 1954; No 13 & 20 in 1956; No 15 & 22 in 1957; No 17 & 21 in 1959; No 23 & 24 in use until broad gauge closed in 1965.
	to				to	
	1921	0-4-0T			24	
3068	1947	0-4-0DA3	3 cylinder 37bhp	F.C. Hibberd & Co 'Planet'	25	Weight 7 tons.
3255/6/7	1948	0-4-0DA3		F.C. Hibberd & Co 'Planet'	26	Nos 28 & 36 broken-up in 1962.
8/9 & 3444	to				to	No 36 exhibited at the Festival of Britain in 1951.
/5/6/7/8/9	1950				36	

The following locomotives are preserved: No 13 at the Talyllyn Railway Museum, Towyn; No 15 at the Irish Steam Preservation Society, Leitrim; No 17 at the Guinness Museum, Dublin; No 20 at the Belfast Transport Museum; No 23 at the Chalk Pits Museum, Amberley, West Sussex.

A. GUINNESS & SON, ST JAMES GATE, DUBLIN (cont'd) (Broad gauge 5ft 3in) Closed 24 May 1965

Works No.	Date	Type	Cylinders/horsepower	Builder	Brewery number/name	Notes
	1912	0-4-0WP	4 cylinder 90hp	Straker & Squire Ltd	1	Petrol-mechanical. Withdrawn 1916, scrapped 1921.
1079	1914	0-4-0ST	15in x 22in o/c	Hudswell Clarke & Co	2	Scrapped in 1965. 'Tramway' skirts fitted all round. 3ft 4in wheels.
1152	1919	0-4-0ST	15in x 22in o/c	Hudswell Clarke & Co	3	Weight when empty 24 tons. Brass bell fitted to Nos 2 & 3. 3ft 4in wheels.
D700	1949	0-4-0D	8 cylinder	Hudswell Clarke & Co	4 'Guinness'	Scrapped 1966. Davey Paxman. Weight 32 tons.

No. 3 preserved by the Railway Preservation Society of Ireland, York Road, Belfast.

	1888	0-4-0	Haulage Wagon	W. Spence, Dublin	1	Cost £450. Weight 8 tons.
	1888	0-4-0	Haulage Wagon	W. Spence, Dublin	2	Cost £450. Weight 8 tons.
	1893	0-4-0	Haulage Wagon	W. Spence, Dublin	3	Cost £450. Weight 8 tons.
	1903	0-4-0	Haulage Wagon	W. Spence, Dublin	4	Cost £450. Weight 8 tons.

No. 4 truck and the hoist used in lifting the narrow gauge locomotives onto these trucks are preserved by the Narrow Gauge Railway Society at the Chalk Pits Museum, Amberley, West Sussex.

Livery: Dark olive green with single red coach line. In 1950 the new house livery of dark blue was used, with red buffer beams. In 1962 the front and rear skirts of the broad gauge locomotives were painted yellow. The diesel No 4 was delivered new in 1949 in the dark blue livery, and after overhaul in 1964 it was outshopped in the familiar zebra stripes of black-and-yellow to the skirts at each end.

A. GUINNESS & SON, PARK ROYAL, LONDON Last remaining brewery railway system, still in use 1982

Works No.	Date	Type	Cylinders/horsepower	Builder	Brewery number/name	Notes
6514	1926	0-4-0WD		Sentinel		Delivered in December. Withdrawn in May 1946.
3270	1948	0-4-0D	144hp	F. C. Hibberd & Co	'Carpenter'	Paxman-Ricardo 6RWT. Delivered in December.
3271	1949	0-4-0D	144hp	F. C. Hibberd & Co	'Walrus'	Paxman-Ricardo 6RWT. Delivered in February.

Livery: Royal blue with single gold coach line and gold Harp logo on cab side sheet; since 1979 yellow lining and logo. Cab inside painted white. Brass nameplates with red background. Red buffer beams and wheels.

IND COOPE, BURTON

Works No.	Date	Type	Cylinders/horsepower	Builder	Brewery number/name	Notes
-	-	0-4-0WT	14in x 20in o/c	Thornewill & Warham		Photographic evidence only.
2022	1885	0-4-0ST	o/c	R. W. Hawthorn Ltd	1	
2295	1895	0-4-0ST	o/c	Hawthorn Leslie	2	Sold to Cowpen Coal Co Ltd, Northumberland in 1927.
2345	1896	0-4-0ST	o/c	Hawthorn Leslie	2	Rebuilt by Thornewill & Warham in 1925. Scrapped in June 1949.
3632	1925	0-4-0ST	14in o/c	Hawthorn Leslie	3	Rebuilt by Baguley into diesel in 1951.
3540	1923		14in o/c	Hawthorn Leslie	4	
533	1922	4WE	Battery 240 volts	English Electric	9	Bought from W. D. Bramley, November 1946.
9376	1947	4WTG	6¾in x 9in 100hp	Sentinel	7	Sold to Thomas Hill (Rotherham) in 1960. Preserved at Quainton Road, Aylesbury.
9384	1948	4WTG	6¾in x 9in 100hp	Sentinel	8	Scrapped in 1970.
3227	1951	0-4-0D	Paxman 150 hp	E. E. Baguley	2	Ex-rebuilt at Romford Brewery in 1955.
3357	1951	0-4-0D	Paxman 150 hp	E. E. Baguley		Weight 22 tons.

IND COOPE LTD, ROMFORD (Rail traffic ceased in 1963)

Works No.	Date	Type	Cylinders/horsepower	Builder	Brewery number/name	Notes
160	1872	0-4-0ST	o/c	Fox, Walker	'Eclipse'	
161	1872	0-4-0ST	o/c	Fox, Walker	'Oscar'	
2345	1896	0-4-0ST	o/c	Hawthorn Leslie	2	From Burton in 1925, Sold in 1927.
2513	1902	0-4-0ST	o/c	Hawthorn Leslie	3	
1142	1908	0-4-0ST	o/c	Peckett & Son	1	Sold to Gravesend Steel & Tinplate Co, Gorsemion, Glamorgan.
3539	1923	0-4-0ST	o/c	Hawthorn Leslie	1	From Burton in 1948. Returned in 1951.
3540	1923	0-4-0ST	o/c	Hawthorn Leslie	3	Sent to Burton in 1937.
2028	1937	0-4-0ST	o/c	Andrew Barclay	5	Scrapped in 1952.
3227	1951	0-4-0D	Paxman 150hp	E. E. Baguley	2	Sent to Burton in 1955. Weight 22 tons.

Livery: Both Burton and Romford Breweries had the same livery of Brunswick green, with a thick black band with a thin straw coach line. Style of company name on locomotives varied, Allsopp added from June 1934, and then dropped in 1958. Hand device used in several forms whilst name incorporated Allsopps. Ind Coope brass rectangular plates with locomotive number and Ind Coope letters on red background.

MARSTON, THOMPSON & EVERSHED LTD, BURTON (Rail traffic ceased in June 1964)

Works No.	Date	Type	Cylinders/horsepower	Builder	Brewery number/name	Notes
2502	1901	0-4-0ST	o/c	R. & W. Hawthorn Leslie	1	Sold to Ford Motor Co Ltd, Dagenham.
2837	1910	0-4-0ST	o/c	R. & W. Hawthorn Leslie	2	Purchased from Herbertsons Ltd, Chollerford, Hexham in 1918. Sold to Priestman Colls Ltd, Co Durham in 1938.
3581	1924	0-4-0ST	o/c	R. & W. Hawthorn Leslie	3	Sold in 1967 for preservation at Shugborough.
3774	1931	0-4-0ST	o/c	R. & W. Hawthorn Leslie	4	Scrapped February 1955. Frame, wheels and nameplate incorporated in Baguley diesel No 3410/4.
3410	1955	0-4-0D	Gardener 150hp	E. E. Baguley	4	Weight 27 tons.

Livery: Deep navy blue with one broad band in sand, one narrow line in orange, broad red line to wheels. British Transport Commission register plates (oval) were fixed below makers' brass plates - Nos 2552 and 2553 dated 1958. Full company nameplate and number stop in brass, with red background.

MITCHELL & BUTLER LTD, CAPE HILL BREWERY, SMETHWICK, BIRMINGHAM (Rail traffic ceased March 1962, Amalgamated with Bass in 1961)

Works No.	Date	Type	Cylinders/horsepower	Builder	Brewery number/name	Notes
117	1889	0-4-0ST	o/c	Manning Wardle	'Beatrice' formerly 'Frank'	Scrapped in 1929.
6369	1907	0-4-0ST	o/c	Aveling & Porter	'John Barleycorn'	Withdrawn in 1951.
1480	1916	0-4-0ST	o/c	Andrew Barclay & Son	'Boniface'	
2307	1951	0-4-0ST	o/c	Andrew Barclay & Son	'John Barleycorn II'	

Livery: Royal blue with straw coach lining.

Works No.	Date	Type	Cylinders/ horsepower	Builder	Brewery number/name	Notes
OAKHILL BREWERY CO LTD, SOMERSET (Narrow Gauge 2ft 6in Closed 1921)						
1701	1903	0-4-0ST	7½in x 12in o/c	W. G. Bagnall	'Mendip'	Delivered in June.
1021	1904	0-4-0ST	9in x 14in o/c	Peckett & Son	'Oakhill'	Delivered in April. In use at the Penarth Cement Works Glamorgan, in 1949.

Livery: Mendip was olive green with black bands, having inner yellow and outer red lines; side rods, connecting rods and buffer beams were vermillion. Oakhill was also olive green with black bands and yellow coach lining; outside frames were painted chocolate-brown with a black border and yellow line. Outside cranks and buffer beams were vermillion. Brass nameplates with red background.

Works No.	Date	Type	Cylinders/ horsepower	Builder	Brewery number/name	Notes
THOMAS SALT & CO LTD, BURTON (closed 1928, acquired by Bass)						
	1869	0-4-0WT		Thornewill & Warham		Scrapped in 1888.
272	1885	0-4-0ST	14in x 20in o/c	Hudswell Clarke	1	Rebuilt by Hudswell Clarke 1923. Sold to Worthington & Co Ltd in 1928. 3ft 6½in wheels.
576	1900	0-4-0ST	14in x 20in o/c	Hudswell Clarke	2	Sold to Wellingborough Iron Co Ltd in 1928. 3ft 7in wheels.
621	1919	0-4-0ST	13in x 18in o/c	E. E. Baguley	3 'Swansea'	Rebuilt by Hudswell Clarke in 1925, Sold to APCM Ltd, Harbury, in 1928. Weight 22 tons.

Livery: Brownish maroon with yellow coach lining.

Works No.	Date	Type	Cylinders/ horsepower	Builder	Brewery number/name	Notes
TRUMAN, HANBURY & BUXTON, BLACK EAGLE, BURTON (closed 1971)						
406	1886	0-4-0St		Yorkshire Engineering Co	None	
2507	1901	0-4-0ST		Hunslet Engineering Co	None	Scrapped in 1954.
1585	1922	0-4-0ST	o/c	Peckett & Son	None	Scrapped in 1955.
2112	1949	0-4-0ST	12in x 18in o/c	Peckett & Son	None	Sold to J C Staton & Co Ltd in March 1958.
2136	1953	0-4-0ST	12in x 18in o/c	Peckett & Son	None	Withdrawn 1965.

Livery: The Pecketts were in that company's standard mid-green, with broad black bands forming panels, with yellow/black/yellow lining. Black footplate and frames, red buffer beams and coupling rods. Locomotives were not allocated brewery numbers or names.

Works No.	Date	Type	Cylinders/ horsepower	Builder	Brewery number/name	Notes
WORTHINGTON & SON, BURTON (Amalgamated with Bass in 1926)						
262	1883	0-4-0ST	14in x 20in o/c	Hudswell Clarke	1	Sold in 1929, to Tyne Tees Shipping Co Ltd. Middlesborough. 3ft 6½in wheels.
	1890	0-4-0ST	o/c	Hudswell Clarke	2	Sold in 1904.
452	1896	0-4-0ST	14in x 20in o/c	Hudswell Clarke	3	Sold in 1958. Renumbered Bass No 12. 3ft 6½in wheels.
602	1901	0-4-0ST	14in x 20in o/c	Hudswell Clarke	4	Sold in 1963. Renumbered Bass No 15. 3ft 6½in wheels.
690	1904	0-4-0ST	14in x 20in o/c	Hudswell Clarke	2	Sold in 1961. Renumbered Bass No 14. 3ft 6½in wheels.
1427	1899	0-4-0ST	o/c	Manning Wardle		Acquired from Burton Brewery Co in 1914. Rebuilt in 1916. Sold in 1926 to Mansfield Standard Sand Co Ltd.
1417	1920	0-4-0ST	14in x 20in o/c	Hudswell Clarke	6	Sold in 1960. 3ft 6½in wheels.
2108	1923	0-4-0ST	o/c	W. G. Bagnall	5	Sold in 1964. Renumbered Bass No 16.
272	1884	0-4-0ST	14in x 20in o/c	Hudswell Clarke	1	Acquired from T. Salt & Co by Bass in 1927, sold to Worthington in 1928.
2815	1945	0-4-0ST	o/c	W. G. Bagnall	1	Sold in 1944.
	1924	0-4-0	40hp Dorman, converted to diesel 1953	Honeywill Bros, Planet	7	Sold in 1963. 3-speed Duplex. Bass No 13. Weight 8 tons.
	1924	0-4-0	Petrol, converted to diesel in 1955	Honeywill Bros, Planet	8	Sold in 1967. 3-speed Duplex. Bass No 17. Weight 8 tons.
	1925	0-4-0	Petrol, converted to diesel in 1957	Honeywill Bros, Planet	9	Sold in 1967. 3-speed Duplex. Bass No 18. Weight 8 tons.
	1926	0-4-0	Petrol, converted to diesel in 1955	Honeywill Bros, Planet	10	Sold in 1967. 3-speed Duplex. Bass No 19. Weight 8 tons.
	1929	0-4-0	Petrol, converted to diesel in 1950	F. C. Hibberd	11	Sold in 1967. 3-speed Duplex. Bass No 20. Weight 8 tons.
	1934	0-4-0	Petrol, converted to diesel in 1952	F. C. Hibberd	12	Sold in 1967. 3-speed Duplex. Bass no 22. Weight 8 tons.

Livery: Dark blue with single red coach line and red buffer beams. Large rectangular brass and red company plate on cab side sheet, with 'sword' motif and date of manufacture.

APPENDIX B : BREWERY & MALTING PRIVATE RAILWAY SIDING LIST

Town and county	Railway Company	Brewery or malting company
Abingdon, Berks	GWR	Morland United Brewery
Aldershot, Hants	LSWR(SR)	Aylwards
Alloa, Clackmannan	NBR(LMS)	Arrol's Brewery
Alloa, Clackmannan		Younger's Ale
Alloa, Clackmannan		Younger's Bottling Stores, Kelliebank
Alloa, Clackmannan		Younger's Maltings
Alloa, Clackmannan		Younger's Old Malt Barns
Alloa, Clackmannan		Grange Brewery
Alloa, Clackmannan		Shore Brewery (J.Calder & Co)
Alloa, Clackmannan		Bass Crest Brewery
Alton, Hants	LSWR(SR)	Alton Brewery
Ashby, Leics	Mid	Burton Brewery
Aylesbury, Bucks	LNWR	Aylesbury Brewery
Baldock, Herts	GNR(LNE)	Pages Malting
Bath, Som	Mid(GW)	Bath Brewery
Barnetby, Lincoln	GC(LNER)	Truswell Brewery
Barnsley, Yorks	GC	Barnsley Brewery
Barnsley, Yorks	GC	Wilkinson's Malt Kiln
Barnwell Junction, Cambs	GE(LNER)	Commercial Brewery (H.A. & D. Taylor Ltd Maltings)
Beeston, Notts	Mid	Beeston Brewery
Bedford, Beds	LMS	Mitchell & Butlers (ex-LNWR)
Bedford, Beds	LMS	Mitchell & Butlers (ex-Midland)
Beverly, Yorks	LNE	Hull Brewery
Bentley, Yorks	Mid	Bentley's Yorkshire Breweries
Birmingham, Warwick	LNWR(LMS)	Mitchell & Butler
Blackford, Lanark	NBR	R. & D. Sharp Ltd
Blyton, Lincoln	GCR	Jeffery's Malt Kiln
Bolton, Lancs	LNWR	Magee, Marshall & Co
Braintree, Essex	GER(LNER)	Braintree Brewery Co
Brackley, Northants	LNWR	Hopcroft & Norris
Brainwith, Yorks	GCR/GNR	Milnthorpe's Malt Kiln
Brentwood, Essex	LNER	Fielder & Co (Malting)
Bridgewater, Somerset	GWR	Starkey, Knight & Ford (Dock Branch)
Bryumawr, Mon	GWR/LMS	Buchan & Co (Rhymney Brewery)
Buckingham, Bucks	LNWR	Aylesbury Brewery Co
Bury St Edmunds, Suffolk	LNER	H.A.& D.Taylor Ltd (Malting)
Bury St Edmunds, Suffolk	LNER	Gough Maltings
Bury St Edmunds, Suffolk	LNER	South Mill Maltings
Buntingford, Herts	LNER	J. & C. Sworder (Maltings)
Burton-on-Trent, Staffs	Mid/LNWR/GNR/ NGR(LMS)	Allsopp & Sons Breweries Guild Street & Hay
		Shobnall Maltings (LNWR) Dallow Lane
		Sidings (LNWR) Horninglow Street
		Sidings (Midland) Station Street & Repton
		Bass & Co Breweries, Bond End, Guild Street, Hay & Sanders Branches
		Shobnall Maltings
		Sidings Station Street & Repton
		Bindley & Co Brewery, Bond End branch (Midland)
		Burton Brewery, Hay & Sanders branches (Midland)
		Charrington & Co, Bond End branch (Midland)
		Cooper & Co, Crescent Brewery, Horninglow branch (Midland)
		Eadie Sidings, Bond End branch (Midland)
		English Grain Co, Station Street & Repton
		Everard & Co, Trent Brewery Bond End branch (Midland)
		Everard & Co, Welcome Sidings
		Evershed's Sidings, Bond End branch (Midland)
		Ind Coope & Co, Shobnall Maltings (Midland)
		Station Street and Branston
		Siding, Mosley Street branch
		Guild Street 'A' Brewery & Maltings

Town and county	Railway company	Brewery or malting company
		Cold Stores and premises
		Curzon Street Maltings
		Dale Street Maltings
		Stables and garages, Sanders branch
		Magee Marshall & Co Brewery, Bond End branch (Midland)
		Marston Thompson & Son's Horninglow Street Maltings (Midland) Guild Street branch
		Passburg Sidings, Station Street and Repton sidings, Shobnall branch
		Cold Storage, Sanders branch
		Park Street Maltings, Bond End
		Meakin's Siding (Midland) Leicester Juct.
		Morton & Co Sidings (Midland) Station Street & Repton
		Peach & Co Welcome Siding, Bond End branch
		Robinson's Brewery (Midland) Bond End brach
		Salt & Co Siding (Midland) Bond End and Hay branches
		Truman, Hanbury & Buxton's(Midland) Station Street & Repton
		Walker & Son's Brewery (Midland) Shobnall branch
		Worthington & Co(Midland)Bond End, Hay and Sanders oranches
		Crown Maltings, Station Street and Branston
		Siding, Station Street and Branson Sidings
Caergw le Castle, Denbigh	WM&CQR	Lassell & Charmans Brewery
Cambridge, Cambs	GER	Commercial Brewery
Cambus, Clackman	NBR(LNER)	Knox's Brewery
Canterbury, Kent	SECR	Makeson's
Cannock, Staffs	LNWR	Blencoe & Co
Cardiff, Glamorgan	GWR/LNWR/TVR (GWR/LMS)	Cardiff Malting Co
Castle Eden, Durham	NER(LNER)	Nimmo & Sons, Brewery
Castleton, Lancs	L&YR(LMS)	Magee, Marshall & Co
Castleford, Yorks	NER(LNER)	T.P. Fawcett (Malting)
Chelmsford, Essex	GER(LNER)	Gray's Brewery
Chelmsford, Essex	GER(LNER)	T.D.Ridley & Sons (Hartford End Brewery)
Chelmsford, Essex	GER(LNER)	W.H.Marriage & Sons (Malting)
Chesterfield, Derby	LMS	Brampton Brewery
Chesterfield, Derby	GCR(LMS)	Tadcaster Brewery
Colchester, Essex	GER(LNER)	Colchester Brewery
Colchester, Essex (Hythe)	GER(LNER)	Truman, Hanbury & Co
Colchester, Essex	GER(LNER)	Groom, Daniels & Co
Colchester, Essex	GER(LNER)	Ind, Coope & Allsopp Ltd
Colchester, Essex	GER(LNER)	Marriage & Sons (Maltings)
Darlington, Durham	LNER	North of England Maltings
Derby, Derbyshire	Mid	Wheeldon's Maltings
Dorchester, Dorset	LSWR(SR)	Eldridge, Pope & Co Brewery
Dublin, Dublin, Eire	GS&WR	A.Guinness Brewery
Dundalk, Louth	GNR(I)	Great Northern Brewery
Edinburgh (Duddingston & Craigmillar)	NBR(LNER)	Murray's Craigmillar Brewery
Edinburgh (Duddingston & Craigmillar)	NBR(LNER)	Deuchar's Brewery
Edinburgh (Duddingston & Craigmillar)	NBR(LNER)	Drybrough's Brewery
Edinburgh (Duddingston & Craigmillar)	NBR(LNER)	Edinburgh Malting Co
Edinburgh (Duddingston & Craigmillar)	NBR(LNER)	Maclachan's Castle Brewery
Edinburgh (Duddingston & Craigmillar)	NBR(LNER)	Paterson's Pentland Brewery
Edinburgh (Duddingston & Craigmillar)	NBR(LNER)	Raeburn's Brewery

Town and county	Railway Company	Brewery or malting company	Town and county	Railway Company	Brewery or malting company
Edinburgh (Duddingston & Craigmillar)	NBR(LNER)	Somerville North British Brewery	Lichfield, Staffs	LNWR(LMS)	Peach & Co (Malting)
Edinburgh, Midlothian	Cal (LNER)	R.Younger & Co (South Leith branch)	Lowestoft, Suffolk	LNER	Maltings
Edinburgh, Midlothian	Cal (LNER)	Great Northern Brewery	London, Middlesex	GWR/LMS/LNER	James Calder & Co Shore Brewery
Edinburgh, Midlothian	Cal (LNER)	McEwan's Fountain Brewery, Merchiston	London, Kensington	Mid	Lovibond & Sons
Edinburgh, Midlothian	Cal (LNER)	Palace Brewery, Rose Lane			
Edinburgh, Midlothian	Cal (LNER)	Lorimer & Clark Caledonian Brewery	Manchester, Lancs	Man Ship Canal	A. Guinness & Son Co Ltd
Edinburgh, Midlothian	Cal (LNER)	Usher & Son Brewery	Manchester, Lancs (dock)	Man Ship Canal	R.& W. Paul Ltd (Malting)
Edinburgh, Midlothian	Cal (LNER)	McEwan's Malt Barns	Milford Junction Street,Yorks	NER	J. Smith's Brewery
Edinburgh, Midlothian	Cal (LNER)	T. & J.Bernards Edinburgh Brewery	Maidstone, Kent	SR	Style & Winch Brewery
Edinburgh, Midlothian	Cal (LNER)	Jefferey & Co Roseburn Brewery	Middlesborough, Yorks	NER(LNER)	Bass & Co Ale Stores
Ely (Landaff) Glamorgan	GWR	Crosswell's Brewery	Mistley, Essex	GER(LNER)	W. Brooks & Sons (Malting)
Eye, Suffolk	GER	Colchester Brewery	Mistley, Essex	GER(LNER)	Edme Maltings
			Mistley, Essex	GER(LNER)	Free, Rodwell & Co (Malting)
			Mirfield, Yorks	LMS	Sutcliffe's, Malt Kilns
Falkirk, Stirling	NB/Cal (LNER/LMS)	Aitken's Falkirk Brewert	Monk Fryston, Yorks	LNER	J. Smith's Brewery Company
Farnborough, Hants	SR	H. & G. Simmonds			
			Neath, Glamorgan	Neath & Brecon (GWR)	Vale of Neath Brewery
Glasgow, Renfrew	Cal (LMS)	McEwan & Son (Buchanan Street)	Newark, Notts	GNR & Midland Joint (LNER & LMS)	Warwicks & Richardson
Glasgow, Lanark	NBR (LMS/LNER)	Phoenix Malting Works			Bishop & Son, Cow Lane Malt Kiln
Glasgow, Lanark	NBR (LMS/LNER)	C.Tennant & Co			Bishop & Son, Spital Malting
					Branston's Maltings
Gloucester, Glos	LMS/GWR	G. & W.E. Downing, High Orchard Maltings			Branston's Riverside Malt Kiln
					J. Hole & Co
Guide Bridge, Lancs	GCR/GNR/Mid (LNER/LMS)	Gartside Brewery			J. Hole & Co Spital Malting
Grays, Essex	LMS	Hugh Baird & Sons (Maltings)			Gilstrap, Earp & Co, Cow Lane Maltings
Grays, Essex	LTSR(LMS)	Seabrook & Sons Brewery			Gilstrap, Earp & Co Maltings (GN)
Gresley, Derby	Mid-LNW	Thompson & Son, Gresley Brewery			Gilstrap, Earp & Co, Massey sidings
Grimsby, Lincoln	GCR(LNER)	Gilstrap, Earp & Co (Malting)			H.Baird, Cliff Nook Kilns
Grimsby, Lincoln	GCR(LNER)	A.Soames & Son			H.Baird, Concrete Kilns No 2 & 3
					H.Baird, Spital Kiln No 1
			Newbury, Bekrs	GWR	H.Baird & Sons Ltd (Maltings)
Halifax, Yorks	GCR	Hall's Malt Kilns	Newport, Mon (Alexandra Dock)	A(N&SW)D&R (GWR)	Phillips & Sons Malt House (Penner Wharf)
Halifax, Yorks	GNR/L&YR	S.Webster & Sons Ltd	Northampton, Notts	LNWR	Northampton Brewery (Western Wharf)
Harleston, Norfolk	LNE	Watney, Combe, Reid & Co (Malting)			
Heckmondwike, Yorks	L&YR(LNER)	Springwell Brewery Co			
Hemingbrough, Yorks	NER(LNER)	J.Smith & Co Malt Kiln (Tadcaster Brewery)	Oulton Broad, Suffolk	LNER	Swonnell & Sons Ltd (Malting)
Hereford, Hereford	GWR/LMS	Watkins Bros			
Hertford, Herts	GNR(LNER)	McMullen's Son			
Hope Village & Cefu-y-bedd, Denbigh	WM&CQR	Lassell & Sharman's Brewery	Panmure, Forfar	Cal/NBR	Tennant & Co
			Park Royal, Middlesex	GWR	A.Guinness & Son
			Penshaw, Durham	NER(LNER)	Tadcaster Tower Brewery
Ipswich, Suffolk	LNER	E.Watkins (Malting)	Peterborough, Northampton	GNR(LNER)	Gilstrap, Earp & Co Paston Siding
Ipswich, Suffolk	LNER	Ipswich Malting Co Ltd (dock)	Peterborough, Northampton	GNR(LNER)	Phillips & Sons Malt House (Malting)
Ipswich, Suffolk	LNER	R. & W. Paul Ltd, (Maltings)	Pengam, Mon	GWR	Pengam Brewery
Inverness	LMS	Walker & Co	Pontypridd, Glamorgan	TVR	Newbridge Rhondda Brewery Co
			Pontefract, Yorks	LMS	W.J.Robson & Co Ltd
Kendall, Westmorland	LNWR	Wnitwell, Mark & Co			
Kilbirnie, Ayr	LMS	Knox's Brewery	Rainford Village, Lancs	LNWR	Birch & Co Brewery
Kimberley,Notts	Mid (LMS)	R.G. Hansons Brewery	Reading, Berks	GWR	H. & G. Simmonds
Kimberley,Notts	Mid (LMS)	Hardy's Brewery	Retford, Notts	GCR/GNR/Mid	Gilstrap, Earp & Co (GC)(Malting)
Kings Lynn, Norfolk	LNER/LMS	Morgan's Brewery Company	Retford, Notts	GCR/Midland	Worksop & Retford Brewery Co
Kings Lynn, Norfolk	LNER/LMS	R. & W. Paul Ltd (Maltings)	Romford, Essex	GER(LNER)	Ind, Coope & Allsopp Ltd
Kircaldy, Fife	NBR(LNER)	Hutchinson & Co Maltings	Royston, Herts	GNR(LNER)	J. & J.E.Phillips Brewery
Kircaldy, Fife	NBR(LNER)	Victoria Maltings (Harbour branch)			
Kirton Lindsey, Lincoln	GCR(LNER)	Gleadell's Malt Kilns			
Kiverton Park, Yorks	GCR(LNER)	Sutcliffe's Malt Kilns	Sawbridgeworth, Herts	GER(LNER)	H.A. & D. Taylor (Maltings)
Kiverton Park, Yorks	GCR(LNER)	Hall's Malt Kilns	Sawbridgeworth, Herts	GER(LNER)	W.Lawrence & Sons (Maltings)
			Sherburn-in-Elnet, Yorks	NER	Leeds & Wakefield Brewery
Ladybank, Fife	NBR(LNER)	Malt Barns Sidings	Shrewsbury, Salop	LNWR/GWR	Jones & Sons Shropshire Maltings
Leamington, Warwick	LNWR	Thomas & Cos Malthouse siding	Sleaford, Lincoln	GNR(LNE)	Bass & Co
Leeming Bar, Yorks	NER	Plews & Sons, Vale of Mowbray Brewery	Snape, Suffolk	GER	Newson Garrett & Son (Malting)
			Stanstead, Essex	GER(LNER)	Maltings
Langwith, Derby	LMS	Peach & Co (Malting)	Starbeck, Yorks	NER(LNER)	Tattersall's Malt Kiln
Leicester, Leicester	Mid (LNW)	Watney, Combe & Co	Stockton-on-Tees, Durham	LNER	Bass & Co Ale Stores
Leith, Midlothian	Cal (LMS)	R. Younger's Malt Barns	Stockton-on-Tees, Durham	LNER	North Riding Maltings
Leith, Midlothian	NBR(LNER)	T. Bernard & Co	Stowmarket, Suffolk	GER(LNER)	R. & W. Paul's (Maltings)
Leytonstone, Essex	GE	Combe & Co	Stowmarket, Suffolk	GER(LNER)	Free & Co (Maltings)
Liverpool, Lancs	LMS	Walkers	Stowmarket, Suffolk	GER(LNER)	Greene, King & Son Ltd
Lichfield, Staffs	LNWR(LMS)	Evans & Co Trent Valley Maltings	Stratford,on-Avon, Warwicks	GWR	Flower & Sons
Lichfield, Staffs	LNWR(LMS)	Ind, Coope & Allsopps Ltd	Stratford, Essex	GER	Ind Coope & Co
Lichfield, Staffs	LNWR(LMS)	Lichfield Brewery	Sudbury, Suffolk	GER(LNER)	Oliver Bros Brewery

Town and county	Railway Company	Brewery or malting company	Town and county	Railway Company	Brewery or malting company
Sudbury, Suffolk	GER(LNER)	Free, Rodwell & Co (Maltings)	Warrington, Lancs	LNWR(LMS)	Walker & Sons (Dallow Lane Branch)
Sudbury, Suffolk	GER(LNER)	Cornards (Maltings)	Watford, Herts	LNWR(LMS)	Benskin's Watford Brewery
Sudbury, Suffolk	GER(LNER)	R. & A. Allen & Son (Maltings)	Watford, Herts	LNWR(LMS)	Wells & Co, Brewery
Sunderland, Durham	LNER	Younger's	West Kensington, Middlesex	Mid	Lovibond & Sons Brewery
Stirling, Stirling	NBR/Cal	McEwan's Malt Barns	Weston, Somerset	Mid (LMS)	Weston Brewery
Stirling, Stirling	NBR/Cal	Aitken's Brewery	Weston, Somerset	Mid (LMS)	Taylor's Maltings
St Margarets, Herts	LNER	H.A. & D. Taylor Ltd (Maltings)	Weston Wharf, Northampton	LNWR	Northampton Brewery Company
Swaffam, Norfolk	LNER	Jeffery's & Co (Maltings)	Wickwar, Glos	Mid	Arnold, Perrett & Co Brewery
			Wigan, Lancs	LNWR(LMS)	J.B. Almond's Standish Brewery
			Wigan, Lancs	LNWR(LMS)	Summer & Co, Haigh Brewery
Tadcaster, Yorks	LNER	John Smith Ltd	Witham, Essex	LNER	Hugh Baird & Sons Ltd (Maltings)
Tadcaster, Yorks	NER	Tadcaster Tower Brewery Company	Woodlesford, Yorks	Mid (LMS)	H. Bentley & Co
Tadcaster, Yorks	NER	Colley's Malt Kilns			Woodlesford Brewery Company
Tewkesbury, Glos	LMS	G. & W.E.Downing, High Orchard Maltings	Woolwich (North) Essex	GER	Bass & Co
Thornton Junct, Fife	NBR(LNER)	Lochty Maltings	Worksop, Notts	LNER/LMS	Worksop & Retford Brewery
Thorpe-le-Soken, Essex	GER(LNER)	Mackenzie, Donald & Sons, later Free Rodwell & Co (Maltings)	Worksop, Notts	LNER/LMS	Sutcliffe's Malt Kilns
Tivetshall, Norfolk	LNER	Watney, Combe, Reid & Co (Malting)	Wolverhampton, Staffs	GWR	W. Butler & Co
Tweedmouth, Northumberland	LNER	J.P. Simpson & Co, Tween Dock Maltings	Wrexham, Denbigh	GWR	Lager Brewery Co
			Yarmouth, Norfolk	GER/M&GN (LNER/M&GN)	Lacon & Co Brewery (GE Tramway)
Warrington, Lancs	LNWR(LMS)	Greenall, Whitley & Co, Wilderspool Brewery	Yeadon, Yorks	LMS	Naylor Jennings & Co, Green Lane Mill
			York	LMS	Yorkshire Breweries Co

APPENDIX C : BURTON BREWERY RAIL CONNECTIONS

MALTINGS

Meakins siding from Leicester Junction in use 9 October 1878. LNWR admitted 22 June 1881. New sidings to new maltings (one of which was occupied by Worthington & Co) although not completed was opened for traffic 12 September 1883.

Peach & Co of Wood Street, siding opened on 10 September 1896, but only small shunting locomotives allowed to enter, such as the Dealey 0-4-0Ts.

BREWERIES

Burton Brewery, High Street began loading own ale 3 February 1863. Its own locomotive, a Manning Wardle, commenced working 3 October 1867. Second locomotive in use from 3 September 1872. Company became absorbed into Worthington's in 1914, brewery by Ind Coope Ltd.

F. Thompson & Son, Horninglow Street began loading own ale 27 May 1865. Mosley Street Branch opened. Siding to its malthouse on the Guild Street opened 19 December 1874. Guild Street siding opened 23 August 1869. LNWR began running into it. Loading began 1 November 1869.

J. Nunneley, Bridge Street began loading own ale 5 June 1865.

Phillips Bros (Truman) began loading own ale 16 November 1865.

T.F.Salt & Co, High Street amalgamated with Clay, Leeson, Greaves & Musgrove. Began loading own ale 30 November 1862, and before locomotives were allowed to cross Anderstaff Lane (6 November 1864) the firm worked its traffic on this side of the lane by horses. Own locomotive used from 25 November 1869. From 1 January 1870 the company commenced working its traffic to and from Midland Railway Junction at Horninglow with its own locomotive. New locomotive shed erected 28 January 1871. Second locomotive in use from 22 January 1873. New signalbox leading to Sales Maltings sidings on Hay branch opened 30 July 1877.

J.Bell & Co, (later Roe & Pickering), Lichfield Street siding leading from Perks & Sons siding on the Bond End branch to its storage premises opened 1 August 1882, on which date the LNWR exercised its right to use the siding. New siding off Bond End extension, at Park Street No 2 into brewery was opened for traffic on 23 January 1888; LNWR access from 17 February 1888.

Staton & Newton extension line from the Shobnall branch to the canal and new ale dock opened for traffic 2 November 1874 (with Mann & Crossman) Siding off the LNWR. Shobnall and Stretton branches opened for receipt of traffic on 1 September and on 5 September 1882 respectively. Midland Railway began to deliver and fetch traffic with its own locomotives.

J.Porter & Son, Dale Street.Siding off Bond End branch opened for traffic 20 October 1882, on which day the LNWR began to use the line.

P.Walker, Clarence Street, Built 1880. Siding from off Bond End branch near Uxbridge Street branch was opened for receipt of traffic on 12 April 1883, from when it was also used by the LNWR. Green & Clarkson's brewery purchased in January 1891.

Sykes & Co, Wood Street. Siding into brewery from Bond End branch opened 28 July 1890, with LNWR having access.

C.Hill & Son, Lichfield Street. Siding off Bond End branch opened for use on 1 July 1879, from which date the LNWR had access. Bond End extension into brewery opened 14 June 1881.

Charrington & Co, Abbey Street. Built 1872. Amalgamated with Meakin's. Siding to the Wood Street malthouses, an extension from the Bond End branch, was opened 18 October 1878. Wood Street stores began loading its ales on 17 March 1880. Siding into brewery opened 8 June 1880. Own locomotive began work on 1 May 1885 over Bond End and Shobnall branches - traffic for the LNWR was taken to that company's Dallow Lane sidings.

T.Bindley, New Street. Bond End extension of line from James Street Junction opened 26 April 1880.

Clayton & Co, Horninglow Road South. Siding from the Midland Railway Horninglow branch opened 1 May 1880.

Truman, Hanbury & Buxton, Derby Street. Built in 1873. Brewery locomotive began to haul the traffic from 1 July 1880. Locomotive shed built at end of main brewhouse.

T.Robinson, Union Street. Bond End extension from James Street Junction, opened siding into brewery 26 April 1880.

T.Cooper & Co, Victoria Crescent. Additional siding into the brewery premises from the Horninglow branch opened 26 October 1874. Midland Railway built a wharf and ale dock near Crescent Brewery in 1882.

Mann, Crossman & Paulin, Shobnall Road. Built in 1874. Albion Brewery. Extension line from the Shobnall branch to the canal and new ale dock opened for goods traffic on 2 November 1874 - extended to Mann, Crossman & Paulin brewery on 29 December 1876. LNWR commenced traffic on Bond End extension on 20 June 1881. Vacated in 1902 and taken-over by J.Marston, Thompson & Son Ltd, which amalgamated with S.Evershed in 1905.

J.Eadie, Cross Street. Siding from the Bond End branch opened 28 November 1877. Worked by Midland Railway locomotives. LNWR worked over maltings siding 10 June 1878. Siding to new cask-washing sheds near Park Street No.1 crossing opened 3 September 1884 - the LNWR had access.

S.Evershed, Bank Square (In 1905 became part of Marston, Thompson & Evershed) Siding off the Bond End branch opened 4 January 1878. LNWR worked over malting siding 10 June 1878. Own loading of ale began on 17 June 1878. Evershed siding into its new premises from the Bond End extension, between Lichfield Street and James Street, opened 1 November 1882, on which day LNWR also claimed its right to use the line.

A.B.Walker & Son, Shobnall Road. Siding leading off the Midland Railway Shobnall branch temporarily opened 19 November 1878. LNWR began to put its traffic into siding 29 November 1878 with its own locomotives. Permanently opened 1 January 1879.

Everard's Brewery Ltd, Anglesy Road. Brewing commenced 1898 at the Trent Brewery, served by two sidings off the Bond End branch from its inception. Leicester Brewery purchased from W.Bates in Southgate Street, Leicester in 1892, but closed in 1931. All brewing continues at the Trent Brewery; rail traffic ceased around 1967.

Index